Turn Great Ideas into Reality: Develop and Present a Winning Business Case

Daniel C. Yeomans, PMI-PMP, PMI-RMP, CMQ/OE

Contributors: Peter Rogers and Alex Wright

Lead Editor: Robert B. Childress

This edition published by
Dog Ear Publishing
4010 W. 86th Street, Ste H
Indianapolis, IN 46268

www.dogearpublishing.net

ISBN: 978-145750-323-8
This book is printed on acid-free paper.

Printed in the United States of America

Table of Contents

Introduction

A Business Case is an essential document or presentation that describes the reasoning to initiate or kill a proposed project or activity. Most Business Cases are normally developed and presented in the form of a well-structured written proposal. However, some Business Cases may be abbreviated and presented in the form of a short verbal argument or presentation. A compelling Business Case adequately captures both the quantifiable and unquantifiable characteristics of a proposed project.

The ability to successfully develop and present a winning Business Case is a difference maker. Successful Business Cases present great ideas that offer opportunities and turn them into reality. Successful Business Cases also ensure that ideas that shouldn't be pursued for a variety of reasons do not reach the project stage and negatively impact an organization. Simply stated, a solid Business Case allows organizations to make the right decisions, at the right time, to pursue the right projects.

The purpose of this book is two-fold. Objective one is to provide you with a comprehensive, understandable, and exportable method to build a powerful Business Case that will be successful. We walk you through each step of the process to ensure you address all key areas thoroughly.

Objective two is to provide best practices and proven methods to present a Business Case to all levels of management to gain ultimate approval. We share proven formats, presentation best practices, and show you how to "win the day." We are confident this book will satisfy both your Business Case preparation and presentation needs.

You may have observed that this book is published as an 8 ½ by 11 inch document. There is reasoning behind this decision. We hope you will use this book as "THE" single source document for developing and presenting your Business Case. Write notes, add highlights, and use this book as a tool to be successful. A "Food for Thought" section is included at the end of all chapters.

We refer to "You" throughout this book. The reason for this is easy to explain. You are the one who will develop and present the Business Case. You are responsible to ensure all key Business Case specifics are addressed. Because *you* are accountable, and we want *you* to be successful—this book is for **YOU!**

This book is dedicated to:

- Every entrepreneur who has a great idea just waiting to happen. Share your idea and make a difference!

- Every intraprenuer who has a vision to improve their organization. Especially to my friends and colleagues at Microsoft Corporation and Becauz LLC. You are empowered!

- Every individual who wants to determine the best path to grow as an individual and contributor to society. Make it happen!

- Every Social Entrepreneur who sees an issue impacting society and the world that needs to be addressed. Make things better!

- Every student who has the "best idea since sliced bread" and wants to water their Professor's eyes with their plan. Here's to your A+!

- My family and friends who put up with me every day. Thank you Chizuko, Yuri, Kyoko, Elsa, Erika, and Josie the dog!

- And especially to the men and women of Northwest University's MBA, Masters in Social Entrepreneurship (MASE), and Leadership Education for Adult Professionals (LEAP) Programs—you inspire myself and others to greater heights!

Forward

It is a great privilege for me to write the forward to Daniel Yeomans' new book, *Presenting and Developing a Winning Business Case*. Dan is one of the most popular adjunct professors at Northwest University, where he has taught in our undergraduate and graduate business programs for many years. Dan has a remarkable ability to simplify complex topics and engage students with even the most challenging subjects.

Some of Dan's initial ideas for this book developed out of a new graduate course he taught for us in 2010, "Project Management for Social Entrepreneurs." As he and I discussed the new course, we realized that there weren't any text materials that applied Project Management principles to the Business Case development process, let alone to the new field of Social Entrepreneurship. This book now fills that gap, and fills it superbly well.

In addition to contributing to the Project Management field, however, this book will be of great value to anyone who wants to learn how to make a convincing Business Case. As with all of Dan's instruction, this text is clear and concise as it walks the reader through the rigorous analysis process required to bring a business or Social Venture idea to reality. I am confident that this book will become the "go to" text in a variety of contexts. As one of our MBA students remarked to me last week, "I always learn something from Professor Yeomans," I know this book will also be a rich learning experience for many.

Teresa Gillespie, J.D., Dean, Northwest University School of Business & Management

Acknowledgements

Nothing in life happens by accident. I would like to acknowledge a few individuals and groups who helped pave the way for the publication of this book.

- **United States Air Force:** In appreciation for the many opportunities to present Business Cases to high ranking decision makers to make our Air Force's communications infrastructure the best!

- **Harry Matthews and Mike Edwards (formerly) of Microsoft Corporation:** Thank you for the opportunity to develop and present challenging Business Cases to executive decision makers for approval many years ago. What a great experience!

- **Cynthia Holmberg and Rick Baker:** Thank you for opportunities to develop multiple iterations of "How to Develop and Present a Winning Business Case" to IT professionals in Microsoft Corporation over the past eleven years. Special thanks to Cynthia—she is my Emergenetics ® mentor, coach, and hero!

- **Northwest University:** Thanks to Dr. Don Doty, Dean Teresa Gillespie, and the many colleagues who encouraged me to bring the art of developing winning Business Cases into the undergraduate and graduate level programs of a great educational institution.

- **Air Force Sergeants Association:** Thanks to a great Association that fights hard to ensure any military member wearing the uniform is provided with a fair and equitable quality of life. We made the case for many great ideas to improve an Air Force member's quality of life, and many of them worked!

- **Becauz LLC:** Thanks to my friends and colleagues for entertaining new ideas to move the company forward!

- **Michelle Young and Microsoft Finance Academy Partners:** Thanks to associates in the Microsoft Finance Academy for a request to develop an end-to-end Business Case curriculum. Your partnership finally convinced me to write the book that had been growing inside of me for years!

- **Seth Goldman and Honest Tea:** Thank you for your consent to use a splendid Mission Statement example from your company!

About the Author

Daniel C. Yeomans

Daniel C. Yeomans brings more than thirty-five years of consulting and leadership experience to his client work. He is a highly proficient and an acknowledged expert as a senior project manager, process manager, business analyst and trainer, delivering over 3,500 seminars and classes in his extensive career. In his years at Microsoft, Dan acquired a thorough understanding of methods used to develop and approve Business Cases. He has applied the Instructional Systems Design model to lead or assist in the development of approximately 40 - 45 Microsoft business skill courses to date. His expertise includes a thorough understanding of common financial metrics used to measure the economic impact of technology on business performance, including Payback, Cost/Benefit Analysis, NPV, IRR, and ROI. A highly competent course development expert, he designed and implemented the majority of project management certification and application courses currently offered in Microsoft IT, and developed the PM Certification Learning Module series for Microsoft IT as well.

Dan's expertise has taken him through the doors of such companies as Microsoft, American Express, Nordstrom, AT&T Wireless, Western Wireless, US Air Force, and Lucent Technologies. An avid learner, Dan holds an MBA from St. Martin's College; a BA in Management from McKendree College; a Project Management Professional (PMI-PMP®) and Risk Management Professional (PMI-RMP®) certification from the Project Management Institute (PMI ®), and a Certified Manager of Quality/Organizational Excellence Certified (CMQ/OE ®) from the American Society of Quality. Dan is also a qualified *Emergenetics* ® Associate.

Contact: dan@becauz.com

About the Contributors

Alex Wright

As a development coach, Alex Wright has more than fifteen years of experience at leading Fortune 100 companies and coaching senior directors, general managers, presidents, and their teams worldwide. His background includes the successful delivery of global systems and support for Human Resources, Leadership Development, Finance, Operations, and Treasury systems. Alex combines his years of business success with a personal passion for unlocking leadership and team potential. His award-winning work has been recognized in industry journals such as Treasury and Risk Magazine, and Directions on Microsoft.

Alex's coaching is distinguished by the use of emotional intelligence, consistency, and kindness to get the most out of people. He's found that even in today's technology-rich work environment, success in business is still based on functional interpersonal relationships.

From his earliest days as a cable TV personality, to living in a remote Eskimo fishing village on the Alaskan tundra, to surviving a near-fatal parachute malfunction, Alex values "measured" risk-taking and embracing change for growth - both of which he calls prerequisites for getting the most out of people and realizing one's own potential. Alex received his education from the University of Washington, with a focus on English and Communications, a degree in Computer Information Systems from Bellevue College and multiple Leadership Development certifications.

Contact: alex@becauz.com

Peter Rogers

Partner of BECAUZ, Peter Rogers combines a strong academic background with his high-impact development expertise to bring out the best in people, their teams, and their organizations. Peter challenges people to choose what and where they want to be, and enables them to thrive in the ecosystems that they impact and mold to their purposes. Peter draws heavily from his advanced degrees in biological and management sciences, policy and economics as he works with people to frame solutions to the most daunting challenges.

Drawing on thirty years of experience, with over twenty of those years as a consultant to Microsoft and other Fortune 100 companies, Peter typically works with leaders and managers in the space between strategy development and strategy implementation to assure that organizations allocate their resources to the work that will deliver on their goals and strategies. He assures that leaders' visions resonate with those who are tasked with delivering on those visions, and causes unproductive behaviors and work to be removed from systems.

Prior to joining BECAUZ, Peter was instrumental in the startup and success of two companies. In a third company, Cell Therapeutics, he served as head of strategic projects, and helped to take this company public on NASDAQ. Peter has been an adjunct professor and guest lecturer at Florida International University and several other colleges and universities. A sought-after speaker, he has spoken at Project World and other conferences.

Peter actively seeks opportunity and is an advocate of the importance of change, risk, and adventure. He is an avid sailboat racer and finds that being of service brings the most meaning to his life.

Contact: peter@becauz.com

About The Editors

Lead Editor: Robert B. Childress

Rob Childress is the primary editor for this book. This is my second book, and the second time I've enlisted Rob's services. Rob has an eye for detail, and provides valued input which leads to many positive changes and additions before we go to print.

Rob is a Senior Master Sergeant in the United States Air Force. He has spent the past twenty years serving his country with pride. Rob has attended every professional leadership school offered by the Air Force and excelled in each. He received numerous awards and accolades for his academic performance.

Rob currently holds an Associate in Applied Science Degree for Transportation Management and an Associate in Applied Science Degree for Instructor of Technology and Military Science from the Community College of the Air Force. He also holds a Bachelor of Science Degree from Hawaii Pacific University with a Major in Business Administration. He is currently pursuing a Master's Degree in Business Administration from Hawaii Pacific University.

Rob is a seasoned facilitator, solid manager, and proven leader. He spent the past few years as the head of an Air Force school that prepares young Air Force members to become tomorrow's leaders.

Rob is married to Shannon Childress, and they reside with their daughter Jessica in Browns Point, Washington. His daughter Brittany lives in Ft. Meade, Maryland. Finally, his daughter Allison is attending Grand Canyon University in Arizona.

Secondary Editor: Robert H. Winkler

Robert H. Winkler is a long-time friend and associate with an amazing eye for detail as well. Bob is a leader in the Air Force Sergeant's Association and Life Insurance industry. He has over 58 years of Life Insurance experience.

Bob is able to review my written thoughts and find the small errors that potentially detract. Bob has proof read many documents for me over the years and made me look good!

Chapter 1: Business Case Basics

The corporate environment is a moving target. Market conditions, customer expectations, technology, and compliance requirements dictate that all organizations recognize opportunities that can move a company forward, and threats that can send it backwards. A Business Case can be developed for many reasons in many forms. Business Cases can be formal, informal, long, or short. They can be documents, presentations, or a verbal elevator pitch. They tell a story that shares an idea, defends why it is important, and presents a plan to grasp an opportunity.

A Business Case is essential if you need to convince others to support, validate, approve, or fund a new project. It is a tool used by both Corporate and Social Entrepreneurs to share great ideas and turn them into reality. The most common instances when a Business Case is required include:

1. **Respond to a downward directed project tasking:** This is a common scenario. Many Business Cases are developed to support goals defined in a corporate portfolio and result from downward generated tasking. The focus of this type of Business Case is on the project's deliverables. You need to show that you understand the expectations of management, and can meet them through your proposal. The focus of the downward directed Business Case is normally on the solution and benefits your organization or companywants to achieve.

2. **Generate a new idea upward:** This is a common scenario as well. Teams and individuals often discover problems and situations that need to be resolved, or opportunities waiting to happen. The focus of this type of Business Case is on the value proposition you share. You must convince decision makers that your idea is worthy of their consideration.

3. **Social Entrepreneurship Business Case:** The majority of guidance provided in this book supports the goals of visionaries who wish to become Social Entrepreneurs. These are people with a vision to eliminate pain or injustice in society today. Chapter 10 addresses additional aspects of a Business Case a Social Entrepreneur needs to consider.

4. **Individual improvement and direction:** Some people develop a Business Case to determine the direction they should take as individuals in both the work and personal environment. This book will not specifically focus on this third type of Business Case. However, we will include a methodology and areas of consideration in Chapter 11.

Components of a Winning Business Case

Every Business Case has key components which must be addressed. Some components are more critical than others. In addition, some components must be well defined before other components can be considered. Figure 1.1 illustrates how a typical Business Case development process should flow. Some components may require emphasis or de-emphasis based on your particular proposal.

Figure 1.1   Business Case Seven-Step Development Flow

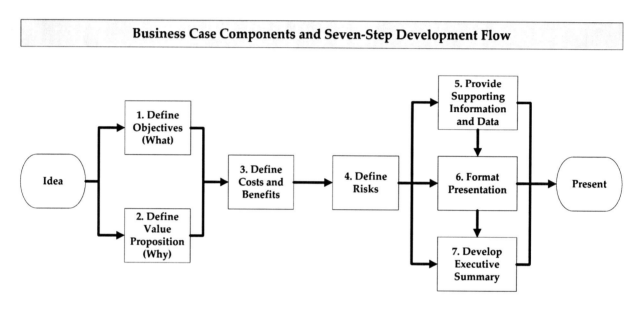

Figure 1.1 is a quick overview of each critical step, and the information you need to include in your Business Case. We need to provide a key clarifier before we move forward. The primary purpose of a Business Case is to allow decision makers to determine if an idea is worthy to move on to the project stage. Some ideas merit approval. Other ideas merit disapproval. A solid Business Case supports good ideas, and stops the bad ones from happening.

A Business Case is not meant to be the final project plan. *Final scope, budget, schedules, etc. will be developed during the project initiating and planning phases after the Business Case is approved.* A solid Business Case allows decision makers to determine if moving to the project phase is warranted.

Business Case Seven-Step Development Flow Overview

Step 1: Define Objectives: This is a critical first-step that must be achieved before moving forward. It is necessary to determine precisely what your objective for the Business Case will be. You may have heard the saying, "First impressions are lasting." This holds true for this step as well. State your objectives, or "What" you propose, and strive to deliver your proposal in straight forward terms.

DO NOT get caught up in the "how" trap. You are not ready to provide a detailed project plan to achieve your objectives at this time. If you attempt to do so, your chances of success will be greatly reduced. Remember—try to sell the decision maker on "What" you propose. Apply the "ABC" model—be accurate, brief, and concise! We will introduce a SMARTWAY model that will assist you in ensuring your objectives are solid in Chapter 2.

Step 2: Define Value Proposition: Defining objectives gets you "in the door." A solid value proposition keeps you there. In reality, you generally develop your objectives and value propositions simultaneously. As the old saying goes, "You can't have one without the other."

During this step, show "Why" your objective(s) need to occur. In most cases, there is an opportunity waiting to happen, a situation that needs to be addressed, or a problem that needs to be solved. Empathy is an interpersonal skill that can help you during this step. Put yourself in the shoes of the decision makers. Try to state your value proposition in terms that have meaning to the decision makers—not just to you. We will introduce two solid models that will help define your value proposition in Chapter 3. These are the Harvard School of Business Balanced Scorecard ® and "FURPS" models.

Step 3: Define Costs and Benefits: Every Business Case should be able to show benefits that outweigh costs. The exception to this rule is when a Business Case must be implemented to address legal or compliance issues. These types of Business Cases are "Must Haves" despite the costs versus benefits breakout.

There are a number of costs you need to consider. In addition, you need to be able to document and distinguish between "hard" benefits and "soft" benefits. We devote Chapter 4 to the cost versus benefit analysis. We also share key financial metrics that may be required, along with some common and useful estimation models.

Step 4: Define Risks: Risk is defined as any cause and event that can potentially impact your proposed idea or project. Risks can be classified as negative if they pose a potential threat. Risks can also be classified as positive if they lead to opportunities. I'm sure this statement raised a few question marks—positive risks? We'll explain the concept of positive risks in-depth later in this book.

It is critical to address risks and list them, preferably using a tool called a "Risk Register." We will cover this important consideration and illustrate an easy to use Risk Register in Chapter 5.

Step 5: Provide Supporting Information and Data: There are a number of other considerations that may need to be addressed in a Business Case. These considerations are often situational based on the type of Business Case you need to present. We address factors such as scheduling, stakeholder management, change management, compliance considerations, etc. in Chapter 6. We also provide some Business Case tools and techniques you may wish to use in Chapter 7.

We also add additional supporting information and data that the Social Entrepreneur may need to consider in Chapter 10.

Step 6: Format Presentation: Formatting your presentation in the optimal way to achieve success is critical. It is important to organize your Business Case presentation in a way that will be understood and compelling. Decision makers expect a presentation that is logical and easy to follow. Chapter 8 is devoted to this subject. We provide formats, templates, and ideas you can use effectively.

Step 7: Develop Executive Summary: Your Executive Summary is a brief synopsis of your Business Case. This summary is normally the first part of your Business Case decision makers read. We end Chapter 8 with an overview of this key component. It is normally a best practice to complete development of the Business Case before finalizing the Executive Summary. This practice ensures you have all the information you require to complete this component available.

Business Case Presentation Overview

Completing the Business Case and satisfying all informational requirements is an important first phase. Next comes an equally challenging phase—the presentation piece. We devote Chapter 9 to effective presentation techniques you should employ. Among the topics we cover are:

- A proven five-step presentation approach that works!

- Effective presentation methods, tactics and tips. We explain how to capture an audience's attention, motivate them to listen, keep their attention through the presentation, leave them with a positive final impression, and close the deal.

- How to deal with questions and tough audiences.

- How to use voice, gestures, body language, and facial expressions to your advantage during the Business Case presentation.

A tabular view of the Business Case development format we use throughout this book is shown in Figure 1.2. This figure lists all key components of a winning Business Case, and serves as a guide as we discuss each component in the chapters that follow.

So congratulations! You have a great idea you believe should be adopted. Let's start at the very beginning and define your objectives. Our mission is to define the overall goal of the Business Case in a way that will capture the attention of the audience, and resonate with decision makers. Chapter 2 awaits us!

Figure 1.2 Sample Business Case Format

Business Case Component	Overview	Considerations
Executive Summary	• Summarizes all key Business Case components	• High-level overview • Your "Elevator Speech" on paper
Objectives	• High-level objective(s)	• Objective statements tailored to the audience. Think action-result • Prioritized list of recommended options. Includes "As Is" option • Shows Linkage/traceability to corporate/organizational objectives • Hierarchical breakout of objectives • Shares applicable scenarios
Value Proposition	• Reasons to approve the Business Case	• Balanced Scorecard areas supported • FURPS criteria supported
Cost/Benefit Analysis	• High-level cost and benefits review with analysis	• High-level costs • High-level benefits • Applicable financial metrics • Rough Order of Magnitude (ROM) • Assumptions
Risks	• Pertinent opportunities and threats	• Applicable risks in the "Risk Register" • Potential responses
Supporting Information and Data	• Situational data based on informational needs of stakeholders	• Change Management Plan • Stakeholder Register • Scheduling considerations • High-level Work Breakdown Structure (WBS) • Legal/compliance considerations • Architectural impact • Post Implementation Tracking Plan • Other options considered • Required sponsorship • Other information as required

Chapter 1 "Food For Thought"

Do you have a great idea waiting to happen? Take a few moments to write down ideas you feel are candidates for a potential Business Case.

Business Case Ideas/Objective(s)

My Notes:

Chapter 2: Define Objectives

Every Business Case needs to begin with a compelling statement of "What." Defining your Business Case objective is a critical first step. You need to determine in your mind, and on paper, what you truly propose to deliver if your Business Case is approved and becomes a project. Your objective should serve as an introduction to your proposal, and a key component of your elevator speech. In essence, a solid objective "gets you in the door." The rest of your Business Case keeps you there.

The best objective states "What" you propose in "ABC" terms. The statement must be *Accurate, Brief, and Concise.* Solid objectives consist of two parts—an action and a result. The action can be to increase, decrease, add, eliminate, improve, delete, etc. The result should be a specific overview of how the action will be accomplished. For example, "Our objective is to improve the efficiency of our internal accounts receivable process by implementing a process improvement project."

Some objectives may be broad or complex. If this is the case, strive to breakdown your objective into hierarchical statements. For example, a process improvement proposal should provide a breakout of the high-level objective and secondary steps. Use of recognized models can add impact and credibility to your Business Case as well. See the example below which uses a common process improvement model called DMAIC.

Improve Efficiency of the Accounts Receivable Process by Implementing a Process Improvement Project
• Define the current process.
• Measure process performance against Critical Success Factors.
• Analyze process variations. Determine root causes.
• Improve the process. Recommend changes.
• Control improvement results. Sustain the gain.

Defining Objectives: Tips and Guidance

- **Writing Objectives**: Objective statements should be constructed in an action-result format as previously described. Develop objective statements that resonate with the audience. Provide them with a "What" statement that is compelling to them. Framing objectives to meet audience expectations is a key to success. *Tip:* You may want to state your objective in a variety of ways to satisfy differing audience needs. For example, a customer may be moved by an objective that may not influence or impact an internal process contributor.

- **Prioritization**: The most successful Business Cases offer three options and recommend one. Options may include a complete solution, a partial solution, and the "As Is" comparison. Other scenarios may lend themselves to proposing two diverse options. Doing nothing is always an option. In addition, it is sometimes the best option. *Tip:* Show how achievement of your stated objectives is an improvement over the "As Is" state if applicable. Conversely, show how the "To Be" may be a worse choice than the "As Is" if applicable.

- **Time Phasing:** Many decision makers are overwhelmed by a large project proposal. *Tip:* Break out the project into smaller phases. Show how the project can be accomplished step-by-step over time. For example, let's use our previous DMAIC example.

Improve Efficiency of the Accounts Receivable Process by Implementing a Process Improvement Project	Time Phasing
• Define the current process.	Project Phase I: January through March 20xx.
• Measure process performance against Critical Success Factors.	
• Analyze process variations. Determine root causes.	Project Phase II: April 20xx.
• Improve the process. Recommend changes.	Project Phase III: May through September 20xx.
• Control improvement results. Sustain the gain.	

- **Traceability:** All objectives should be linked with corporate or organizational goals and objectives. *Tip:* Show how achieving your objective or proposed project fits into the big picture of what the corporation or organization needs to achieve. Your project should support a valued program. The program should support an organizational strategic planning goal. Ensure the connection between planning goal, program, and project.

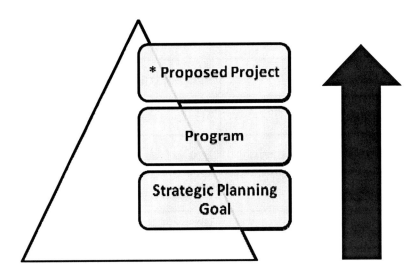

- **Tell a Story:** The best objectives share the "What" of the Business Case in a way that adds meaning. Share your objective as a story or scenario to capture your audience and move them into action. Show where the organizations is, where the organization needs to be, and identify the gaps. *Tip:* Visuals, storyboards, etc. are great methods to express or support an objective.

The "SMARTWAY" Model

The SMARTWAY model is a tool you can use to determine if your objective is worth pursuing. All components of the SMARTWAY model need to be addressed in a Business Case. If you cannot address each component, you may want to delay presentation of your Business Case until you can find all the answers. Figure 2.1 provides an overview of the SMARTWAY model.

Figure 2.1 SMARTWAY Model

SMARTWAY Component	Key Considerations
S: Specific	Accurate, brief, and concise. No ambiguity.
M: Measureable	Project deliverables are measurable.
A: Attainable	Project can be achieved in current environment.
R: Relevant	Project traces back to organizational goals.
T: Target Driven	High-level schedule can be defined.
W: Worth Implementing	Project has a solid value proposition.
A: Assignable	Capacity and required skills are available.
Y: Yields Results	Probability of achieving benefits is high.

"SMARTWAY" Defined

Your initial SMARTWAY evaluation should provide you with the information you need to move forward, postpone, or kill your Business Case. Each SMARTWAY component must be addressed in the Business Case to maximize chances of success. Areas you are unable to address become potential risks that may be the difference between success and failure.

It is important to note that a SMARTWAY evaluation can provide you with justification to recommend disapproval of an idea that shouldn't happen. Remember that the high-level goal of developing a Business Case is to approve great ideas, or stop bad ideas from becoming projects that do more harm than good. Let's expand on the SMARTWAY definitions.

- **Specific:** Your objective should state a specific action and result in simple terms that are understood by the audience segment you are addressing. Ambiguity is the enemy. If the audience needs to translate your objective, or if the objective is not clear, your first impression may be negative and lasting. Share your objective with representative stakeholders from key groups to ensure it makes sense to them. All stakeholders should share a similar interpretation of the objective.

- **Measurable:** You need to ensure your project objectives are measurable. You need to be able to draw a picture of what a successful project outcome looks like. If possible, use measures that reflect the "As Is" state, and contrast it to a "To Be" state target that has meaning to the audience. For example, "We are confident that improving our accounts receivable process will reduce the time required to execute the process by 10%, and reduce time required to collect receivables by 20%."

- **Attainable:** You need to ensure that the project can be accomplished in the current environment. The current environment is impacted by economic circumstances, legal and compliance realities, technology, cultural and social considerations, internal and external politics, and physical/logistical factors. For example, proposing a new project that will require additional headcount during a period when hiring is frozen may not be the best approach.

- **Relevant:** You need to show how your project fits in the overall corporate or organizational big picture. You need to strive for traceability. How will the measurable deliverables from your project support the overall corporate or organizational vision and/or portfolio? How will your proposed project "move the dial" positively on the organizational scorecard?

- **Target Driven:** You need to be able to show how the results you deliver will impact the corporation or organization in a timely manner. Time-phased deliverables may also be an approach to consider if your project is complex and has multiple steps you must achieve to be successful. For example, a promise to deliver needed functionality two months after it is needed will not resonate positively in any decision makers mind. In addition, proposing total project completion within an unrealistic timeframe will also result in lost credibility, questions, and possible disapproval of the Business Case.

- **Worth Implementing:** The value proposition of your Business Case is the second most important statement you will make. The first question decision makers need answered is "What do you propose?" This is satisfied by your objective statement(s). The second question they will ask is, "Why should I care?" We will address this question extensively in Chapter 3. However, if you cannot determine the value of your proposal at a high-level initially, you need to revisit the Business Case's purpose, or start working on an alternative idea.

- **Assignable:** All ideas are dependent upon our most important organizational resource—people. Do you have the necessary capacity and skill sets required to deliver on your Business Case proposal? Is your proposal important enough to warrant trade-offs from other competing projects? Will the proposed project team be motivated to the point where they will embrace the project as their own? These are all considerations that can dictate an initial Go/No-Go decision.

- **Yield Results:** Many Business Cases make great benefit claims they can never keep. Set a goal of making reasonable claims that the project you propose can deliver. In addition, outline a plan on how you will track and prove that the benefits promised were actually achieved. This will increase both credibility and chances of approval. We discuss a "Post Implementation Tracking Plan" later in Chapter 6.

Define Objectives Summary

We discussed defining objectives and provided a "SMARTWAY" model you can use to determine the merit of your Business Case before expending time and energy on next steps. Do you have a solid objective? Are you confident it satisfies SMARTWAY criteria?

If so, we are ready to jump into Chapter 3. If not, refine your objectives, or brainstorm potential alternative objectives to find an idea that is a winner. You told decision makers "What" you proposed in your objective. It is now time to let them know "Why" they should care.

If you need additional ideas, Figure 2.2 provides a list of common actions that are used to define objectives. Each listed action can be accomplished in a number of ways. For example, we could avoid planned costs by achieving a number of results such as reducing scope, eliminating headcount, or achieving efficiencies.

Figure 2.2 Common Business Case Actions to Support Objective Statements

Actions to Support Objective Statements
Avoid Planned Costs (Cost Avoidance)
Conform/Satisfy Legal Requirements
Enable/Improve Service Level Agreement (SLA) Compliance
Enable/Ensure Mandatory Compliance
Implement Process Mapping/Project Definition
Implement Training to Improve Skills
Improve Automation—Reduce Manual Activities
Improve the Customer Partnership Experience (CPE)
Improve Organizational Core Competencies/Skills
Improve Employee Morale and Passion
Improve Process Efficiency (Time & Resource Consumption)
Improve Product/Service Quality
Improve Teamwork and Productivity
Improve Work Life Integration (Work Life Balance)
Improve/Re-engineer Core Process
Increase Organizational Competitive Advantage
Increase Cost Savings/Reduce Costs
Increase Customer Satisfaction (CSAT)
Increase Earnings per Share (EPS)

Actions to Support Objective Statements
Increase Effectiveness
Increase Net Satisfaction (NSAT)
Support Portfolio/Program Goals
Increase Revenue/Sales/Market Share
Increase Stakeholder Adoption
Increase Voice of the Customer (VOC) Interaction
Leverage Employee Skills
Promote Creativity
Reduce Complaints (Internal and External)
Reduce Process Resource Requirements (Tied to Efficiency)
Reduce Process Time (Tied to Efficiency)
Respond to Negative Risks (Threats)
Respond to Positive Risks (Opportunities)
Satisfy Shareholder Expectations

Chapter 2 "Food For Thought"

Try to brainstorm some potential Business Case objectives. Remember the action-result combination to best define an objective. For example: "Increase stakeholder adoption by implementing a user training program." The action is increasing adoption. The result is a new user training program.

Business Case Objectives (Action-Result)

My Notes:

Chapter 3: Define the Business Case Value Proposition

Every idea or investment has an opportunity cost. Decision makers may need to adopt your proposal at the expense of choosing other options. When choices are necessary, opportunities to achieve benefits from projects not chosen are forfeited. It is critical to show that your proposal offers greater opportunity than others in a competitive environment. The best way to achieve this goal is to show as much value as possible. Let decision makers know "Why" your Business Case proposal is a must!

Robert S. Kaplan and David P. Norton created a tool called the "Balanced Scorecard ®."[1] The model has been adopted by CEOs and corporate leaders around the world as indicative of objectives a business organization or corporation needs to satisfy to sustain a business and grow. The Balanced Scorecard is an excellent model that can be used in a Business Case to show multiple reasons "Why" a project should be undertaken. Figure 3.1 shows the four interlocking components of the Balanced Scorecard.

Figure 3.1 Balanced Scorecard Model

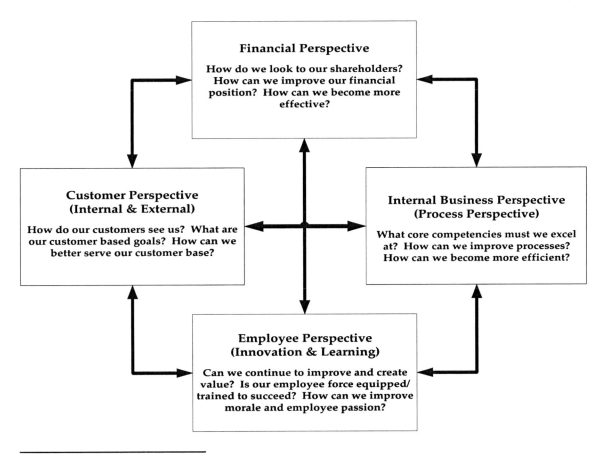

---

[1]Harvard Business Review on Measuring Corporate Performance, Harvard Business School Press

The Balanced Scorecard Model

The Balanced Scorecard model components include a financial perspective, internal business or process perspective, employee or innovation and learning perspective, and a customer perspective. All perspectives must be satisfied and balanced for a business to thrive. You should not sacrifice one or two perspectives to improve a single perspective. This will equate to short-term gain for long-term pain.

Some Business Cases may enhance one of the four components. However, others may enhance multiple components. If you want to increase the chances your Business Case will be approved, the more components your Business Case supports—the better! If you want a Business Case to be disapproved, show how the objective fails to support any of these perspectives, or supports them minimally compared to competing projects. Figure 3.2 shows how the Balanced Scorecard perspectives are a consideration in the daily operations of most organizations or corporations.

Figure 3.2 Balanced Scorecard Process Interface Model

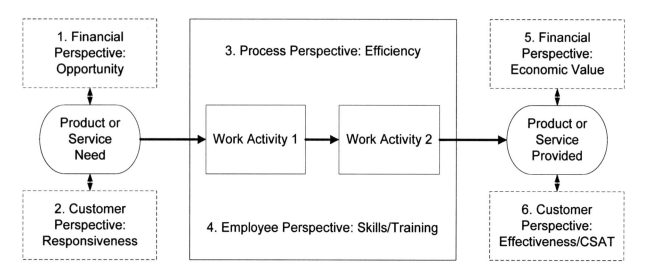

A Business Case normally proposes a new product or service. Here is a quick breakout of how the Balanced Scorecard interacts with the end-to-end process of making a new idea a reality. We use our prior example of "Improve the efficiency of our internal accounts receivable process." Note the numbering used in figure 3.2 tracks directly to the numbers used to describe the interactions on the following page.

1. **Financial Perspective: Opportunity:** Any opportunity that improves overall service in a corporation impacts the financial perspective. Improved service allows an organization to look better in the eyes of their shareholders, and positively impacts the economic bottom line directly or indirectly. Accounts receivable is a process that turns customer promises into needed cash. Improving this critical corporate process yields valuable benefits in multiple areas.

2. **Customer Perspective: Responsiveness:** New product or service ideas should relate to a customer need. Customers may submit formal requests, or let us know when change is needed through their feedback. Customers may be internal or external. In our example, improving the accounts receivable process should be a response to known issues or shortfalls impacting the current process. Addressing these issues is a huge statement to your clients or customers that you heard their voice—and are responding.

3. **Process Perspective: Efficiency:** Products and services must be efficiently planned, developed, and provided. Efficiency is a measure of providing required deliverables in the fastest time possible, while expending the minimum amount of resources. Resources are defined as cash expenditures, human resource levels of effort, and consumption of materials and supplies. Anytime you improve efficiency, you add value to the company or organization. The goal of all organizational and corporate core processes is to implement them as efficiently as possible. The time required to provide a valued deliverable to a customer is a Critical Success Factor. Increased efficiency often improves overall customer satisfaction.

4. **Employee Perspective: Skills and Training:** Efficiency is dependent upon two key variables. Variable one is defining your process in terms that all key stakeholders can understand. The second, and equally important variable, is equipping your number one resource to be successful. That resource is your people. A Business Case may propose an objective to improve the skills and competencies of the people who implement a process as planned. A simpler objective may be to provide better definition around inputs, activities, or key process outputs. Trained and competent employees who understand the objectives of the process, and are competent to perform, execute process activities faster and cheaper. In addition, trained employees are far more confident and proficient. There are fewer questions to be answered, and fewer issues to resolve. There are fewer complaints from stakeholders because the job is being done right. Creativity peaks as employees look for new ways to improve performance.

5. **Financial Perspective: Economic Value:** The product or service you provide is what you sell to customers to enhance the bottom line. A Business Case that improves a product or service normally translates to increased sales, profitability, or output. In our example, improving the accounts receivable process may lead to improved collection percentages, faster collections, less lost revenue, etc. This is a big economic win!

6. **Customer Perspective: Effectiveness and Customer Satisfaction (CSAT):** CPE is a business term which translates to the "Customer Partnership Experience." CPE has two key variables. The first variable is to provide a product or service that meets the customer's needs. We will provide a five-part model that defines "customer needs" later in this chapter. A second variable is service related. Customers want partners to address their issues and concerns in a timely and *effective* manner. It can be argued that effectiveness is a measure from the customer's viewpoint of how well an organization or corporation manages and satisfies their expectations. Effectiveness impacts the customer perspective, and is a key financial perspective driver. In our example, improving an inefficient accounts receivable process may have a positive impact on overall CPE. That is a value proposition worth pursuing.

The examples just discussed are not exclusive. There are many factors in each of the four Balanced Scorecard perspectives to consider. We close out the discussion with an in-depth explanation into each of the four perspectives.

The Financial Perspective

The financial perspective is arguably the one of the most important components of the Balanced Scorecard. The primary goal of every business is to earn enough income to sustain operations and grow. This holds true for both profit and non-profit driven businesses. The financial perspective supports this business reality. Without adequate capital, your business will fail in the long run.

Figure 3.3 provides a breakout of potential value you can share in your Business Case that supports the financial perspective.

Figure 3.3 Balanced Scorecard Financial Perspective

Value Proposition	Brief Description
Compliance/Legal	Ensure key compliance or legal requirements are met. Reduce risks of non-compliance. Mitigate legal issues.
Cost Avoidance	Eliminate the need to spend funds allocated in the budget. Eliminate prior approved projects no longer required.
Cost Savings	Reduce the real costs of doing business. These savings are "bookable." They reduce your budget.
Earnings per Share (EPS)	Increase overall corporate Earnings per Share. Place corporation into a positive light from an investor standpoint.
Effectiveness	Improve corporate products or services to the satisfaction of your customer base (Ties into Customer Perspective).
Increase Revenue	Increase revenue through additional sales, market share, etc. Take advantage of market opportunities.
Risk Management (Opportunities)	Take action to initiate events that may lead to opportunities. Enhance probability and impact of achieving opportunities.
Risk Management (Threats)	Reduce the causes, probability, or impact of potential risks that could require a funds outlay or reduce revenues.
Portfolio/Program Support	Implement projects that allow the business to accomplish documented mission, vision and goals.
Satisfy Shareholders	Implement projects key shareholders deem as having value. Respond to shareholder requests. Listen to the Voice of the Customer (VOC).

The Internal Business or Process Perspective

The internal business or process perspective is a target rich environment for Business Cases in every organization. The focus of this component is on the internal processes used to produce the products and services the customer values. Figure 3.4 provides a breakout of potential value you can share in your Business Case that relates to the internal business or process perspective.

Figure 3.4 Balanced Scorecard Internal Business or Process Perspective

Value Proposition	Brief Description
Automation	Automate a manual process. Goal is to improve time and reduce resource requirements.
Competitive Advantage	Improve the competitive advantage of your organization as compared to external competitors. Gain an edge.
Core Competencies	Improve key core competencies and skills essential to your organization to maintain a competitive advantage.
Efficiency	Present ideas that allow the organization to work smarter. Process improvement initiatives aim to improve efficiency.
Improve Quality	Present ideas that reduce waste, eliminate workarounds, lower amounts of warranty work, etc.
Process Improvement	Present ideas that allow an organization to improve overall process performance (See reduce time/resources below). This includes individual and multiple dependent processes. Implement Total Quality Management (TQM).
Process Mapping	Define and document key processes critical to success of an organization. Improve and share knowledge and understanding of core processes.
Reduce Process Time	Achieve "Lean" goals or opportunities by reducing time to perform key processes.
Reduce Process Resource Requirements	Reduce number of resources required to implement core processes. Enhance overall productivity.
Service Level Agreement (SLA)	Propose projects that will allow an organization to better meet and exceed in-place or proposed SLA with key partners.

The Employee or Innovation and Learning Perspective

The employee or innovation and learning perspective is a Balanced Scorecard component that acknowledges the need for well-trained and motivated employees who help an organization sustain and grow. Figure 3.5 provides a breakout of potential value you can share in your Business Case that relates to the employee or innovation and learning perspective.

Figure 3.5 Balanced Scorecard Employee or Innovation and Learning Perspective

Value Proposition	Brief Description
Adoption	Proposals that capture employee ideas and feedback lead to higher levels of motivation, buy-in, and performance.
Creativity	Creative employees add value. Employee surveys note the freedom to be creative and apply individual talents as a key reason people stay with an organization or company.
Leverage Employee Skills	Projects that allow employees to leverage their skills to a greater extent add value by improving morale and motivation. This often leads to higher retention rates and productivity.
Morale and Passion	Some projects have potential to improve employee morale and passion for the job. Look for win-win scenarios that add value and satisfy employee desires.
Teamwork	Positive team building creates an environment of trust and improves performance. Some projects enhance teamwork, and enable employees to become productive faster.
Training	Training that enables or improves skills and core competencies critical to organizational success is value added.
Work Life Integration	Some projects enhance overall employee Work Life Integration which leads to increased morale and creativity. Work Life Integration is sometimes referred to as Work Life Balance.

The Customer Perspective

The customer perspective is the final component of the Balanced Scorecard model. This perspective acknowledges that the relationship with customers is a key Critical Success Factor that drives an organization or business forward. If there are no customers, there is no profit. Without positive cash flow, all other components really do not matter in the long run. Figure 3.5 provides a breakout of potential value you can share in your Business Case that relates to the customer perspective.

Figure 3.6 Balanced Scorecard Customer Perspective

Value Proposition	Brief Description
Complaints Management	Proposal addresses customer complaints and proposed solutions to reduce or eliminate customer shared issues.
Customer Satisfaction (CSAT)	Project has potential to increase CSAT scores. CSAT is a key measure of customer satisfaction.
Customer Partnership Experience (CPE)	Project addresses key areas of customer service and product/service issues. Proposes improvements.
Net Satisfaction (NSAT)	Project has potential to increase customer NSAT scores. NSAT is a key measure of customer satisfaction.
Voice of the Customer (VOC)	Proposal implements an "Ask" from a key partner or customer. Addresses formal or informal requests. Surveys are a key source for VOC feedback.

Quantifying the Customer Partnership Experience (CPE)

The Customer Partnership Experience (CPE) is a measure of customer satisfaction. As we shared previously, the two primary areas of concern are levels of customer service and product/service viability in the customer's eyes. Any Business Case that enhances levels of customer service is a potential winner. Quantifying product or service expectations requires additional explanation. The "FURPS" model is used by many product and service developers to explain five critical concerns of customers when it comes to purchasing decisions. Your ability to tie your proposal to any or all of these areas will improve chances of successful Business Case adoption. Let's define the FURPS model.

The "FURPS" Model

Customers have choices. They choose partners who offer the best CPE. FURPS addresses a product and/or service criterion that drives purchasing decisions. If a Business Case addresses shortfalls, or proposes improvement opportunities in any of these components, the value of the Business Case increases.

Figure 3.7 "FURPS" Model

Component	Brief Description
Functionality	Customers want products and services that provide the functionality they need to be successful. They expect products that are flexible, scalable, and sustainable. A successful partner understands their key customer's functionality needs, and work diligently to ensure what they are offering matches the specific needs of the customer. As the old saying goes, "If you build it, they will come."
Usability	Many businesses offer great products with multiple features. However, if customers are not aware of the functionality your product or service offers, or if they don't know how to access the functionality, then your attractiveness as a partner is lessened. Increasing usability from the customer standpoint adds value.
Reliability	Customers have expectations for the reliability your product offers. They expect the product or service to provide the expected functionality they need, when they need it. Understanding customer reliability expectations, and addressing shortfalls, is of tremendous value. Meet and exceed customer expectations!
Performance	Performance is a measure of the time required by a customer to access the functionality offered by a product or service. Understand the customer's time/performance constraints, and address shortfalls. This promise will add great value to your Business Case as well. Again, meet and exceed the customer's expectations.
Supportability	Another key consideration in the customer's purchasing decision is supportability. If they need assistance, will it be available? How much are the after purchase costs? Do they need to hire a support team, or will one be provided? Will support be timely? Know the customer's needs and address them. You'll win the day!

Define the Business Case Value Proposition Summary

"What" you propose in a Business Case captures the attention of decision makers. The "Why" factor in your proposal keeps their attention, and allows you to share additional details as required. Here are some keys to success to keep in mind.

- **Balanced Scorecard:** The Balanced Scorecard is acknowledged by business leaders as four key perspectives that must all be met if a business hopes to attain and sustain success over the long-term. Match the objectives of your Business Case to any and all of the four perspectives.

- **Economics 101:** There are two ways to enhance the financial bottom line--sell more products, or reduce costs. Does your Business Case impact these factors?

- **Effectiveness:** Effectiveness is a measure of product or service performance from the customer's viewpoint. Simply speaking, customers partner with effective businesses. Effectiveness translates into revenue and profit.

- **Efficiency:** Efficiency is a measure of how well we build our products and services. Lack of efficiency translates into wasted effort. Highlight the value proposition of objectives that allow an organization to go lean (reduce time required to complete processes), and reduce resource requirements (people, equipment, supplies, materials).

- **Employees:** Employees are an organization's number one resource. Show how your Business Case enhances the employee experience in your organization.

- **Customer Partnership Experience (CPE):** CPE is defined as a businesses' ability to provide great customer service, and/or great products and services. Objectives that enhance CPE are huge potential winners.

- **FURPS:** The FURPS model outlines five buyer considerations when making a product or service selection. Determine if your Business Case addresses shortfalls or opportunities to improve your product or service. Customer testimonials provide great supporting data for value statements in this area.

Value Proposition Checklist

Use this checklist as a guide to inventory your Business Case's value proposition.

Perspective	Considerations	Yes or No
Financial	• Compliance/Legal	
	• Cost Avoidance	
	• Cost Savings	
	• Earnings per Share (EPS)	
	• Effectiveness	
	• Increase Revenue	
	• Risk Management (Opportunities)	
	• Risk Management (Threats)	
	• Portfolio/Program Support	
	• Satisfy Shareholders	
Internal Business or Process	• Competitive Advantage	
	• Core Competencies	
	• Efficiency	
	• Improve Quality	
	• Process Improvement	
	• Process Mapping/Definition	
	• Reduce Process Time	
	• Reduce Process Resource Requirements	
	• Service Level Agreement (SLA)	
Employee or Innovation and Learning Perspective	• Adoption	
	• Creativity	
	• Leverage Employee Skills	
	• Morale and Passion	
	• Teamwork	
	• Training	
	• Work Life Integration	
Customer Perspective	• Complaints Management	
	• Customer Satisfaction (CSAT)	
	• Customer Partnership Experience (CPE)	
	• Net Satisfaction (NSAT)	
	• Voice of the Customer (VOC)	

Chapter 3 "Food For Thought"

Choose an objective for a Business Case. Brainstorm value proposition possibilities supporting the four components of the Balanced Scorecard.

Objective:	
Financial Perspective	Internal Business or Process Perspective
Customer Perspective	Employee or Innovation and Learning Perspective

My Notes:

Chapter 4: Define Costs and Benefits

The financial perspective of the Balanced Scorecard underscores the importance of revenue and cash flow to the sustainment and growth of any business. This chapter introduces three key areas of discussion you likely need to address in your Business Case. How much is the initial cost estimate? How does the initial revenue outlook from proposed benefits appear? When we compare costs to benefits, does moving forward seem feasible?

Let's begin this chapter with an important qualifier. The level of accuracy expected in a Business Case is a Rough Order of Magnitude (ROM) estimate. A ROM level estimate is +/- 50% of what you estimate will ultimately be the actual costs of the project you are proposing. If you estimate the ROM to be $100,000, you are essentially stating you believe the actual cost of the project once planned and executed will ultimately fall within the $50,000 to $150,000 range. More definitive estimates do not occur until the Business Case is approved and the idea becomes a formal project.

Defining Costs

There will likely be costs associated with your project. We begin our discussion with information you need to know to address cost factors in your Business Case.

Direct and Indirect Costs

The two primary cost categories are *direct costs* and *indirect costs*. These categories are explained below.

- **Direct Costs**: Direct costs are funds you must pay. Subcategories of these costs are *fixed costs* to pay product or service set-up or lease fees, and *variable costs* which are based on production.

- **Indirect Costs**: Indirect costs are also costs incurred by a project. However, these costs are not listed as cash requirements in your budget. For example, if two members of your team are salaried workers, you generally do not have to budget for their salaries and benefits. However, these are costs that will be incurred by the project unless the team members are willing to work for free. ☺

CAPEX and OPEX Funding/Cost Categories

Some businesses break out cost categories based on the type of asset being purchased. Two common cost categories you may encounter are Capital Expenses (CAPEX) and Operational Expenses (OPEX). The distinction between these two categories is defined below.

- **CAPEX:** CAPEX funds are used to purchase buildings, equipment, or other assets with a long life. In most cases, assets purchased with CAPEX funds are subject to depreciation. We will define and review depreciation when we discuss benefits later in this chapter. In general, CAPEX funds are used to *attain* new capabilities.

- **OPEX:** OPEX funds are generally used to support the operational costs of running a product, business, or system. In general, we can say OPEX funds are used to *sustain* the business. They are generally included in the annual operating budget.

Cost Categories

There are a number of potential costs you need to capture in a Business Case. Some costs are incurred up-front before any production or services begin. These are referred to as initial investment costs. Other costs are incurred as the project unfolds. These are recurring or operational costs. Both costs must be captured in the Business Case. We provide financial models later in this chapter that highlight this concept.

Here is a key tip to remember. It may be a good idea to develop a schedule that shows project funding requirements phased over time. It is often not practical to request and expect all funds required up-front at the beginning of a project. Phased funding can also improve the overall financial metrics you often need to share, and improve the value of your Business Case.

Figure 4.1 provides a comprehensive list of cost categories that may impact your Business Case. This list is not all inclusive. Use this list as a guide to get you started.

Figure 4.1 Potential Cost Categories

Cost Category	Definition
Contingency Funds	Reserves set aside to accommodate risk events. These are generally Contingency Reserves for known risks. 10% is generally the norm.
Development/ Construction	Costs associated with developing or building the product or service proposed in the Business Case. These may be CAPEX, OPEX, or a combination of these two types of funds.
External Support	Costs to procure external resources needed to achieve objectives of the Business Case. May include external vendors, web support, marketing, advertising, etc.
Hardware	Any hardware, software, or fixed equipment assets required to implement the proposed project. This is normally a CAPEX cost.
Internal Support	Costs incurred to pay for team and other internal Subject Matter Experts. Costs are indirect if they are not part of the project budget. They are direct costs if part of the budget.
Licenses and Permits	Any costs associated with licensing or permit requirements. Could include legal, regulatory, or compliance related fees as well.
Materials/ Supplies	Costs incurred for any consumable materials or supplies needed to implement the proposed project. May include books, tools, etc. These are OPEX costs that may be incurred prior to project initiation, and as the project is being planned and executed.
Support	Any costs incurred at completion of the project. These are normally OPEX costs that must be added to operating budgets. Costs may include all resource categories. Total Cost of Ownership (TCO) or Life Cycle Costing models include costs for after-project support.
Training	Costs incurred to provide key stakeholders with required competencies and skills to plan, execute, and support the product or service.
Travel	Costs to pay for project related travel costs.

Defining Benefits

We discussed potential value propositions for Business Cases in Chapter 3. It is now time to quantify those benefits. An ultimate goal of a successful Business Case is to show that benefits exceed costs. There are two categories of benefits you need to address in your Business Case. Both are critical to success. The two types are referred to as *hard* and *soft* benefits.

Hard Benefits

Hard Benefits: These benefits are normally priority one for decision makers. Hard benefits are also referred to as *bookable* benefits. These benefits provide additional working capital by increasing cash assets, or reducing cash liabilities. Figure 4.2 provides a breakout of potential hard benefits to consider in your Business Case.

Figure 4.2 Potential Hard Benefits

Benefit Category	Definition
Additional Revenue	Cost benefits such as increased sales, quantifiable increases in market share, etc. There is a direct impact on working capital and net income.
Compliance	Some companies include benefits that enable compliance in the hard benefits category. Others may include them in the soft category.
Cost Avoidance	Any benefit resulting in the elimination of a previously funded initiative. For example, we can cancel the ABC project planned cost of $50,000 if we approve this Business Case.
Cost Reduction	Any benefit that allows you to reduce operating expenses in your budget. This could include reduced vendor requirements, lower Cost of Goods Sold (COGS), reduced material/supply needs, fewer returns and warranty work, less scrap, etc. Keep in mind that management will reduce budgets when this type of Business Case is approved.
Headcount	Some projects may result in an ability to reduce headcount in the organization. This is a hard benefit. Staffing reductions are a potential benefit that must be well communicated prior to approval.

Soft Benefits

Soft Benefits: These are benefits that do not directly translate to increased cash flow, or the potential to reduce operating costs in the organization's budget. These benefits include increased morale, productivity, time savings, customer satisfaction, reduced risk, etc. It is difficult to place a direct cash value to these benefits. However, they are tangible benefits that can impact the corporate "bottom line" in a positive way. Figure 4.3 provides a breakout of potential soft benefits to consider.

Figure 4.3 Potential Soft Benefits

Benefit Category	Definition
Customer Service	Some projects increase an organization's ability to provide top-notch customer service. This leads to improved customer satisfaction, and potentially sales. Customer service is part of the CPE equation.
Employee Development	Business Cases that improve skills and competencies lead to improved morale, productivity, initiative, creativity, and employee longevity. It is difficult to quantify actual economic advantages to the bottom line.
Morale and Work Climate	Some Business Cases propose solutions offering potential to increase morale. This leads to greater employee longevity, productivity, etc.
Process Time	Reducing process time is a key benefit from a Business Case. We classify this as a soft benefit as productivity from time savings cannot be guaranteed. Productivity Return on Investment (PROI) can be calculated by multiplying average time savings by the average employee wage.
Resource Reduction	Reducing the number of resources required to execute a core process is another solid benefit. It is optimal to show how reduced resource requirements translate into performing additional workload that could not be accomplished prior to implementation of the project.
Risk Reduction	Reduction of risk can lead to reduced expenditures for mistakes, liabilities, etc. This is not a bookable cost and falls within the soft benefits category. Risk is a potential event. A Business Case may aim to ensure positive risk events occur, and/or negative risk events do not.

Key Financial Metrics Supporting the Business Case

Quantifying the costs and benefits from your Business Case is the first step. Understanding how to represent this data in a manner meaningful to decision makers is an important next step.

We close our discussion on "Defining Costs and Benefits" with an overview of key financial metrics and other considerations you may need to apply to your Business Case. Here is a brief overview of financial metrics and subjects we address in this section.

Subject	Overview
Cash Flow Diagram	Tabular overview of the time-phased costs and benefits forecast for a proposed project. Serves as a basis for development of multiple financial metrics and statements.
Payback	Financial metric that does not consider the total life of a project. Payback calculates how long it will take to recover the initial investment cost, and can be measured in years, months, or days. For example, a project invests $100,000; Payback would calculate the length of time required for revenue to equal $100,000.
Return on Investment (ROI)	Financial metric that provides a percentage evaluation of a project's cash flow. Considers revenue and expenses. Does not consider the Present Value of Money.
Internal Rate of Return (IRR)	Financial metric that provides a percentage evaluation of a project's cash flow. IRR compares the Net Present Value of costs to the Net Present Value of benefits as funds are paid out (costs) or accrued (benefits) over time.
Net Present Value (NPV)	Financial metric that provides positive or negative cash value to evaluate the merit of a project. NPV applies a discount rate to all costs and benefits as they are paid out or accrued over time. A positive Net Present Value normally leads to project selection.

Subject	Overview
Depreciation	Equipment and assets lose value as you use them. In business, you are able to claim lost value of assets you purchase to reduce the amount of taxes your organization must pay. The value lost on an annual basis is called depreciation.
Program Evaluation and Review Technique (PERT)	Program Evaluation and Review Technique: A form of Three-Point Estimating that uses a weighted method to calculate cost and benefit entries based on pessimistic, most likely, and optimistic estimates.
Expected Monetary Value (EMV)	Method used to establish Contingency Reserve requirements for both budget and schedule. EMV is quantified by multiplying probability times the best or worst case cost/time scenario.

Setting up the Cash Flow Diagram

A Cash Flow Diagram must be developed to analyze and share the financial merits of a Business Case. Figure 4.4 shows a simple Cash Flow Diagram we will use for discussion.

Figure 4.4 Sample Cash Flow Diagram

Business Case Financials Illustration 1			
Setting Up a Cash Flow Diagram			
	Costs	Benefits	Total
Investment	($100,000)	$0	($100,000)
Year 1	($15,000)	$50,000	$35,000
Year 2	($5,000)	$75,000	$70,000
Year 3	($55,000)	$100,000	$45,000

- In this Cash Flow Diagram example, we show an initial investment of $100,000 required up-front to start the project.

- In year 1, there are operational costs of $15,000 that will be incurred. However, there is $50,000 forecast in benefits. The result is $50,000 minus $15,000 or $35,000.

- Year 2 and Year 3 have similar scenarios. There are combinations of operating costs and benefits that result in positive cash flow at the end of both years.

- Tip: Be realistic when claiming benefits. Some projects may begin realizing benefits from Day 1. Other projects may take longer. Be able to explain your rationale for the costs and benefits timing depicted in the Cash Flow Diagram.

Calculating Payback

Payback is a financial metric used as a measure of project merit by most corporations and organizations. Some managers refer to Payback as the breakeven point.

It is noted by financial managers that Payback is the worst financial metric to use to determine the economic feasibility of a long-term project. However, Payback reflects the reality of project funding. There are times when no funding for a solid Business Case is available. Decision makers borrow from the current budget to fund the project, but must get that money back before the end of the budget year.

There are two reasons for stating Payback is the worst financial metric you can use to justify a long-term project. Here is the rationale.

- Payback does not consider the total life of a project. It is a metric that calculates how long it will take to recover the initial investment cost and can be measured in years, months, or days. Returns after Payback is achieved are not a consideration.

- Payback also fails to consider the Present Value of Money. Let's use the US dollar to explain this point. If I have a dollar in my hand today, it will buy the equivalent of one dollar's worth of value. However, that same dollar in my hand on a future date will not provide the same value as it does today. Currency loses value over time due to numerous factors such as inflation, growth, etc. As a case in point, one dollar bought far more in 1940 than it buys today.

Figure 4.5 uses our previous cash flow example to show how Payback works.

Figure 4.5 Calculating Payback

Business Case Financials Illustration 2			
Calculating Payback			
	Costs	Benefits	Total
Investment	($100,000)	$0	($100,000)
Year 1	($15,000)	$50,000	$35,000
Year 2	($5,000)	$75,000	$70,000
Year 3	($55,000)	$100,000	$45,000

1. **Step 1:** To calculate Payback, first determine how much your initial investment is. In this example, your initial investment is $100,000.

2. **Step 2:** The next step is to determine when Payback occurred. In Year 1, you netted $35,000. You did not achieve Payback. You need an additional $65,000 to reach the $100,000 investment mark ($100,000 minus $35,000 = $65,000).

3. **Step 3:** At the end of Year 2 you earned $70,000 ($75,000 - $5,000 = $70,000). Add this to the $35,000 you earned in Year 1 and you now have $105,000. You exceeded your $100,000 investment somewhere between the end of Year 1 and the end of Year 2.

4. **Step 4:** Now to the calculations. How much was needed in Year 2 to achieve payback? The answer is $65,000 as we shared in Step 2. How much revenue was gained in Year 2? The answer is $70,000 as shown in the Cash Flow Diagram. When did we achieve Payback?

   o **Here is the calculation:** Divide the amount required to achieve Payback ($65,000) by the amount received in Year 2 ($70,000). The result is approximately 0.93. Payback occurred approximately 93% into year two. We add 1.00 + 0.93 to equal 1.93. Payback took 1.93 Years.

   o You can change this number to days as well. The traditional accounting year has 360 days. If we multiply 1.93 times 360, we can state that Payback will take approximately 695 days to achieve.

Improving Payback: There are two ways to improve Payback. One method is to spread out costs over time. Reducing the amount of your original investment reduces the amount needed to achieve Payback. The second method is to try to increase up-front cash flow. There may be a way to trade-off later year cash revenues for higher early year returns.

Calculating Return on Investment (ROI)

Return on Investment (ROI) is a popular financial metric used to compare unlike projects. For example, an organization may need to choose between investing in a new facility or Information Technology project. ROI levels the playing field, and calculates straight cost and benefit amounts without bias.

ROI provides a percentage result that can be improved in two ways. ROI increases if you can improve total benefits or reduce total costs. Figure 4.6 uses our previous Cash Flow Diagram example to show how ROI is calculated.

Figure 4.6 Calculating ROI

Business Case Financials Illustration 3			
Calculating Return on Investment (ROI)			
	Costs	Benefits	Total
Investment	($100,000)	$0	($100,000)
Year 1	($15,000)	$50,000	$35,000
Year 2	($5,000)	$75,000	$70,000
Year 3	($55,000)	$100,000	$45,000
TOTALS	($175,000)	$225,000	

1. **Step 1:** Calculate all costs for the project. The initial investment plus all additional yearly costs amount to $175,000.

2. **Step 2:** Calculate the total benefits for the project. Total benefits amount to $225,000 over the life of the project.

3. **Step 3:** Apply the formula (Benefits-Costs/Costs). The amounts we place into the formula reflect total costs and benefits ($225,000-$175,000)/$175,000). The result of this calculation is .2857. This decimal translates to 28.57%. It is a best practice to round all percentages used to present any financial metric such as ROI to the nearest hundredth of a percent.

Calculating Internal Rate of Return (IRR)

Internal Rate of Return (IRR) is a key financial metric that considers the Present Value of Money. IRR provides a percentage value that can be used by decision makers to choose projects providing the greatest monetary value. Many corporations use the "Rule of 20%" to determine the merit of project proposals that will be approved solely based on the monetary value they provide. Any project that does not promise greater than 20% IRR is disapproved unless there are extenuating circumstances.

IRR looks at the Net Present Value of costs and compares it to the Net Present Value of benefits as funds are paid out (costs) or accrued (benefits) over time. If the Net Present Value of benefits is greater than the Net Present Value of costs, the project reflects a positive IRR. If the Net Present Value of costs is greater than the Net Present Value of benefits, the project reflects a negative IRR. Strive for the highest IRR you can get to enhance Business Case approval potential.

Figure 4.7 uses the previous Cash Flow Diagram example to show how IRR is calculated. This calculation uses Microsoft Excel to automatically calculate IRR based on the costs and benefits as reflected over the course of the project. There are alternative software applications that calculate IRR as well.

Figure 4.7 Calculating IRR

Business Case Financials Illustration 4			
Calculating Internal Rate of Return (IRR)			
	Costs	Benefits	Total
Investment	($100,000)	$0	($100,000)
Year 1	($15,000)	$50,000	$35,000
Year 2	($5,000)	$75,000	$70,000
Year 3	($55,000)	$100,000	$45,000

1. **Step 1:** The key data needed to calculate IRR is listed in the "Total" column on the Cash Flow Diagram example.

2. **Step 2:** IRR is calculated by comparing the Net Present Value of all investment costs to the Net Present Value of the benefits as shown in the Cash Flow Diagram. In this example, benefits are accrued over a three year period.

3. **Step 3:** IRR is calculated as a percentage. In this example, IRR = 22.31% as shown in the table below. This project barely satisfies the "Rule of 20%" criteria previously shared. However, the IRR is positive. This reflects a positive monetary value.

	Calculating Internal Rate of Return (IRR)	Analysis/Calculations
Formula	Microsoft Excel Solution/Financial Formula (IRR)	22.31%

Improving IRR: You can increase your IRR percentage in the same two ways we discussed in the Payback summary. Reduce early year costs or increase early year benefits to improve the IRR percentage.

Calculating Net Present Value (NPV)

Net Present Value (NPV) is recognized by financial managers as the best metric to use when determining the long-term value of a project. NPV uses the same methodology as IRR with two exceptions.

- NPV provides a currency amount as an answer when calculated. A positive currency amount represents a project that should be undertaken if monetary value is the primary criteria. A negative currency result indicates that the project should not be taken if currency value is the top consideration. Again, note that some projects may be mandatory regardless of the NPV value.

- NPV requires you to input a Discount Rate (sometimes referred to as a Cost of Capital Rate) that is used to calculate the Net Present Value. The lower this rate, the higher the NPV returns. The higher the rate, the lower the returns. NPV uses this rate to "discount" returns. Hence the name—Discount Rate.

Figure 4.8 uses the previous Cash Flow Diagram example to show how NPV is calculated.

Figure 4.8 Calculating NPV

Business Case Financials Illustration 5			
Calculating Net Present Value (NPV)			
10% Discount Rate	Costs	Benefits	Total
Investment	($100,000)	$0	($100,000)
Year 1	($15,000)	$50,000	$35,000
Year 2	($5,000)	$75,000	$70,000
Year 3	($55,000)	$100,000	$45,000

1. **Step 1:** The key data needed to calculate NPV is the "Total" column on the Cash Flow Diagram example. This was true for IRR as well.

2. **Step 2:** Determine the Discount Rate. In this example we use 10%.

3. **Step 3:** NPV calculates the Net Present Value of all investments and benefits accrued over time. NPV uses the 10% discount rate to perform calculations. The result is a cash value.

	Calculating Net Present Value	Analysis/Calculations
Step 1	Discount Rate	10%
Step 2: Formula	Microsoft Excel Solution/Financial Formula (NPV)	$21,344

The $21,344 dollar figure represents the value of this project over a three-year period when a 10% discount is applied to all costs and benefits as depicted in the Cash Flow Diagram. The $21,344 represents the present value of the project. Translated—approval of this project will yield the equivalent of $21,344. The valuation is based on what I could purchase if I had $21,344 in my possession today.

Let's look at a second example at a 12% Discount Rate. NPV is reduced based on this higher value. The project is still positive and worthy of approval. However monetary value is reduced.

	Calculating Net Present Value	Analysis/Calculations
Step 1	Discount Rate	12%
Step 2: Formula	Microsoft Excel Solution/Financial Formula (NPV)	$17,039

Increasing NPV: The formula to increase NPV is the same as we shared for Payback and IRR. Reduce early year costs or increase early year benefits.

Key Financial Metrics Summary

- **Cash Flow Diagram:** Try to set up a simple Cash Flow Diagram to serve as a basis for all calculations. Remember that your estimates are at the ROM level which has a +/- 50% variation.

- **Estimating Methods:** There is an estimating methodology called Program Evaluation and Review Technique (PERT). We model this estimating method for you at the end of this chapter. We also introduce Expected Monetary Value (EMV). EMV is used when the probability of incurring a cost, or achieving monetary benefits, is variable or less than 100%.

- **CAPEX:** CAPEX investments can claim depreciation. Depreciation increases cash flow. We provide a brief overview of depreciation in our last section of this chapter as well.

- **Payback:** Payback is the worst financial metric to use for a long-term project funding decision. However, many decision makers require a Payback analysis be performed as many projects are funded using current budget resources. Payback can be reported as years, months, or days.

- **ROI:** ROI is a simple calculation that is best suited when comparing unlike investment opportunities such as a construction or Information Technology project. ROI provides a percentage response, and can be positively impacted by increasing benefits or reducing costs. If ROI is used to determine the merit of a Business Case, always choose the project with the highest ROI percentage.

- **IRR:** IRR is a widely accepted financial metric that considers the Present Value of Money. It provides a percentage response. Always choose the project with the highest IRR percentage. You can improve IRR by reducing early year costs, or increasing early year returns.

- **NPV:** NPV is acknowledged as the best financial metric to use for a long-term project funding decision. It provides a currency value as a response. A positive NPV value represents a project that should be accepted. A negative NPV value represents a project that should not be accepted. If you are comparing projects, always choose the project with the highest NPV regardless of time. Time is already factored into the calculations. You can improve NPV by reducing early year costs, increasing early year returns, or reducing the Discount Rate.

- **Discount Rate:** NPV must be accompanied by a Discount Rate that is determined by the organization. Discount Rates are normally developed by adding the Cost of Capital + Cost of Equity (% Stockholders expect as ROI) + Range of estimated costs and benefits. *To illustrate:* You are investing $100,000 to develop a new software application to be used to automate portions of your accounts receivable function. You had to use dollars from a short-term loan and prior common stock sales. You suspect a range of +/- 5% for your cost and benefit estimates.

  - **Cost of Capital for the Short-Term Loan:** 4.00%

  - **Expected Return from Stockholders:** 3.50%

  - **Range of Estimates:** 5.00%

  - **Discount Rate:** 4.00% + 3.50% + 5.00% = 12.50%

Defining Cost and Benefits: Other Topics

Depreciation is a source of cash you can claim in your Business Case. In addition, your method of cost estimating can add to your level of cost and benefit estimate accuracy. We address these two additional topics before moving on to the next chapter which addresses risk.

Depreciation

Equipment and assets lose value as you use them. In business, you are able to claim lost value of assets you purchase. The value lost on an annual basis is called depreciation. Figure 4.9 illustrates the cash value of depreciation.

Figure 4.9 Cash Value of Depreciation

Business Case Financials Illustration 6			
Calculating Value of Depreciation			
	Scenario 1	Scenario 2	
Income	$100,000	$100,000	**Cash Value =**
Depreciation	($10,000)	$0	**Depreciation Value x Tax Rate**
Earnings Before Taxes	$90,000	$100,000	
Taxes at 30%	($27,000)	($30,000)	**$10,000 x 30%**
Cash Value of Depreciation	$3,000		**= $3,000**

- In Scenario 1 we earned $100,000. We are able to depreciate an asset at a rate of $10,000 annually. We subtract that amount from our income before we pay taxes. The reduction of depreciation results in earnings of $90,000. At a 30% tax rate, our taxes amount to $27,000.

- In Scenario 2, we have no depreciation to claim. As a result, we pay taxes on our $100,000 of income, and our tax bill amounts to $30,000 at a 30% tax rate.

- Compare Scenario 1 and 2. By claiming depreciation, we paid $3,000 less in taxes than we did without depreciation. If you develop a Business Case where depreciation is a factor, compute the economic benefit of depreciation each year by multiplying the amount you can depreciate ($10,000) times the tax rate (30%). The result: ($10,000 x 30% = $3,000). (Note there are various depreciation models to include straight-line and accelerated methods. Work with your financial team to determine the most appropriate model to use.)

Cost and Benefit Estimating

Cost and benefit estimating is challenging. Estimating accuracy can be improved by using a form of Three-Point Estimating referred to as PERT. The PERT acronym stands for *Program Evaluation and Review Technique.* The premise behind PERT is simple. Statistical studies show that most cost estimates follow a normal distribution. Our most likely estimate occurs approximately 4 out of 6 times. Our best case or optimistic estimate occurs once in six times. Our worst case or pessimistic estimate occurs once in six times as well.

The normal distribution curve is also referred to as the "Bell Curve." A normal distribution curve uses averages and *"Sigma"* intervals to show the potential range of values over the length of the curve. Figure 4.10 provides an illustration.

Figure 4.10 Normal Distribution Curve and Probabilities

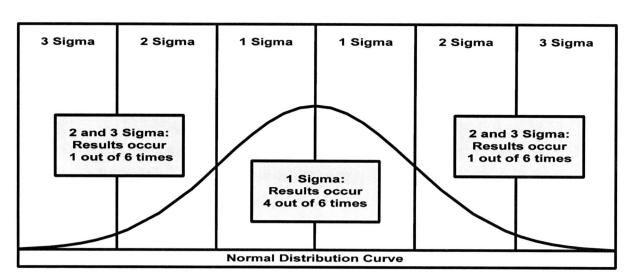

PERT is a weighted form of the Three-Point Estimating method and provides a calculation to determine a revised estimate we can use in our Business Case. Figure 4.10 provides an example illustrating PERT.

PERT: Program Evaluation and Review Technique

Figure 4.11 Estimation Using PERT

Business Case Financials Illustration 7			
Estimation Using PERT			
Estimate	Amount	Multiplier	Sub-Total
Pessimistic	$138,000	1	$138,000
Most Likely	$100,000	4	$400,000
Optimistic	$75,000	1	$75,000
Total		6	$613,000
PERT	Total/6		$102,167

1. The pessimistic, most likely and optimistic estimates for a project are shown. We can assume these figures are based on real data available to the Business Case developer.

2. PERT states that the pessimistic estimate occurs 1 in 6 times. We weight the pessimistic estimate with a multiplier of 1. The result: $138,000 x 1 = $138,000.

3. PERT states that the most likely estimate occurs 4 in 6 times. We weight the most likely estimate with a multiplier of 4. The result: $100,000 x 4 = $400,000.

4. PERT states that the optimistic estimate occurs 1 in 6 times. We weight the optimistic estimate with a multiplier of 1. The result: $75,000 x 1 = $75,000.

5. To calculate the PERT, we add up all weighted estimates ($613,000) and divide by 6. The result we use as our estimate is $102,167.

Some Three-Point Estimating models simply average the pessimistic, most likely, and optimistic values to calculate an estimate. This method is not as accurate as the PERT method.

The PERT form of Three-Point Estimating is far more accurate than One-Point Estimating. One-Point Estimating uses the most likely entry without considering the optimistic and pessimistic values. A One-Point estimate generally has a 10-15% chance of being accurate. Consider Three-Point Estimating using PERT whenever possible.

Expected Monetary Value (EMV)

Expected Monetary Value is another estimating method that can be applied to a Business Case. EMV is used when the probability of incurring a cost, or achieving monetary benefits, is variable or less than 100%. EMV is a primary tool used in Decision Tree Analysis which is defined in the Glossary.

The two key pieces of information you need to use EMV are the probability of incurring a cost or monetary benefit, and the actual cash amount that applies. For example, if you expect there is a 50% chance you will need to purchase a permit for $100, the EMV would be calculated as (50% x $100 = $50). Figure 4.12 provides two examples of EMV for discussion.

Illustration 8 shows how EMV can be used to estimate a scenario where there are various probabilities of an optimistic, most likely, and pessimistic cash value occurring.

Illustration 9 shows how EMV can be used to calculate a cash value when you have multiple costs and benefits with various probabilities of occurring.

Figure 4.12 Estimation Models Using EMV

Illustration 8

Business Case Financials Illustration 8			
Estimation Using Expected Monetary Value I			
Estimate	Amount	Probability	Sub-Total
Pessimistic	$138,000	20%	$27,600
Most Likely	$100,000	40%	$40,000
Optimistic	$75,000	40%	$30,000
Total		100%	$97,600
EMV	Weighted Average		

Illustration 8 Notes

1. This EMV model uses Three-Point pessimistic, most likely and optimistic estimates. Unlike PERT, you determine probabilities for each of the estimates occurring. For example, we assume the 40% optimistic estimate is based on accurate data available to you. The same logic is true for the pessimistic and most likely estimates.

2. The math is relatively easy. Multiply each estimate times the probability. For example, the pessimistic estimate is calculated as $138,000 x 20% = $27,600.

3. Add all sub-totals to calculate your final estimate ($27,600 + $40,000 + $30,000 = $97,600). The $97,600 dollar figure is what you document in your Business Case as your estimate. It is recommended you share your estimating methodology if requested to do so. This support should be included in your Business Case. In addition, be prepared to show how you determined probability percentages.

Illustration 9

Business Case Financials Illustration 9			
Estimation Using Expected Monetary Value II			
Factor	Amount	Probability	Sub-Total
Cost 1	($55,000)	15%	($8,250)
Cost 2	($110,000)	75%	($82,500)
Cost 3	($21,000)	60%	($12,600)
Cost 4	($44,500)	25%	($11,125)
Benefit 1	$120,000	80%	$96,000
Benefit 2	$75,000	40%	$30,000
Total			$11,525
EMV	Cumulative Total		

Illustration 9 Notes

1. This EMV model aggregates multiple costs and benefits to calculate a bottom line estimate. You can use this model for strictly costs or benefits, or to calculate a combination of both as shown.

2. The math is straight forward. Multiply each estimate times the probability. For example, Cost #1 shows ($55,000 x 15% = ($8,250). The parenthesis in this example shows this as a debit or cost. Conversely, numbers not in parenthesis show credits or benefits.

3. Add all sub-totals to calculate your final estimate. In this case, the value of all costs and benefits using EMV is $11,525.

Define Costs and Benefits Final Thought

Cost and benefit estimates are often impacted by risk. Our next chapter discusses the concept of risk, and shares how to integrate this key consideration into your Business Case. Take a few moments to think about the costs and benefits for your Business Case.

Chapter 4 "Food For Thought"

Choose an objective for a Business Case. Brainstorm potential costs, hard benefits, and soft benefits supporting your objective.

Objective:	
Costs (Direct and Indirect)	Potential Hard Benefits
	Potential Soft Benefits

My Notes:

Chapter 5: Define Risk

Risk is defined in the *PMBOK ® Guide*[2] as "an uncertain event or condition that, if it occurs, has a positive or negative effect on at least one of the project's objectives." Project objectives are defined as scope, time, cost, and quality. Every Business Case has risks that need to be identified and dealt with. This section discusses risk, and provides guidance to address this important consideration in your Business Case.

Risk Overview

Risk has three components. Causes lead to risk events. Risk events lead to impacts. A basic model used to explain and describe risk is called *risk meta-language*. Figure 5.1 defines these three components.

Figure 5.1 Risk Components

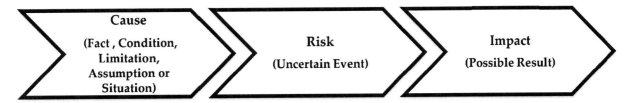

Normally a single cause can lead to multiple risk events. Each risk event can have one or more impacts. Interestingly enough, not all risks are negative. Some risk is actually positive. Here are some examples.

- **Negative Risk or Threats:** A common cause of risks is the method of deriving cost estimates. We can label the cause as "Cost estimating methodology." There are a number of potential events resulting from this cause. A common event scenario posing a threat could be "May result in actual costs running higher than expected." We can list multiple impacts. The most likely would be "This event could limit the features or functionality we can provide to our customers." Putting it all together, we can define the risk as, "Cost estimating methodology may result in actual costs running higher than expected. This event could limit the features or functionality we can provide to our customers."

---

[2] Project Management Body of Knowledge *(PMBOK) ® Guide*, 4th Edition

- **Positive Risks or Opportunities**: Believe it or not, some causes and events can lead to a positive impact or opportunities if they occur. We refer to these events as positive risks. We can use the same cause-event-impact scenario as we did for the negative risk example, and turn things around in the Business Case's favor. For example, "Precise cost estimating methodology may result in more accurate estimates that will allow us to provide 100% of the functionality requested by our customers."

It is important to look for negative events that can lead to threats that impact your Business Case. Negative risks prevent us from achieving our Business Case objectives. It is also advantageous to look for positive events that may lead to opportunities. Positive risks allow us to meet, and sometimes exceed, the objectives of the Business Case.

We need to discuss one final note on risk before we discuss common risk causes and effects to consider. There are two categories of risk. Risk practitioners label these as *known* and *unknown* risks. If we identify a risk, it is referred to as a known risk. If we know about a risk, we can address it in our Business Case, and show decision makers we have done our due diligence.

If we don't know about a risk, it is referred to as an unknown risk. These risks, when they occur, catch us by surprise. This is not good! When presenting your Business Case, you may be asked about your risk analysis methodology. If a decision maker makes you aware of a risk you did not consider, you may lose some credibility. So the bottom line lesson is simple. Do your best to identify as many risks as possible to ensure you are prepared to address this key area during your Business Case presentation.

Common Risk Causes and Effects to Consider

In Chapter 3, we introduced the Balanced Scorecard as a tool to show the value proposition of your Business Case. We now need to analyze potential Business Case value propositions in terms of risk potential. What are causes and potential events that may threaten our value proposition? What are causes and potential events that may help us to meet and exceed our Business Case objectives? These lists are generally referred to as Risk Breakdown Structures (RBS).

As you review these Risk Breakdown Structures (RBS), you may note that a primary objective of your Business Case is to reduce the threat of a negative risk or accentuate a positive risk to achieve an opportunity. Let's revisit the four areas of the Balanced Scorecard, and share common causes and events that may impact, or even drive, your Business Case.

Financial Perspective Risks

Figure 5.2 lists potential financial perspective risks to consider. Most causes of risk offer both threats and opportunities. This RBS is not all inclusive. There are other potential events that could result from each cause listed. However, we hope you can this RBS as a guide to help you identify potential risks impacting your Business Case.

Figure 5.2 Financial Perspective Risks

RBS: Financial Perspective Risks		
Cause, Fact, Condition	**Potential Negative Events**	**Potential Positive Events**
Benefit Estimate	May not be able to achieve forecast benefits.	May be able to exceed forecast benefits.
Budget Constraints	Allocated funds may be issued with constraints.	Allocated funds may be issued with no constraints.
Budget Size	Proposed budget may exceed preliminary forecast.	Proposed budget may be less than originally anticipated.
Compliance/Internal Controls	Solution fit may not meet corporate compliance, or internal control requirements.	Solution fit may enable corporate compliance, or satisfy internal control objectives.
Cost Controls	Planned method to report and control costs may not meet corporate needs.	Proposed cost control system may be viewed as a plus by decision makers.
Cost Estimates	May exceed preliminary cost estimates.	May be able to reduce preliminary cost estimates.
Financial Metrics	May not be able to portray positive IRR and NPV.	May be able to exceed expected IRR and NPV.
Funding Commitments	Business may not follow through on funding commitments.	Business may meet or exceed original funding commitment.

RBS: Financial Perspective Risks Continued		
Cause, Fact, Condition	**Potential Negative Events**	**Potential Positive Events**
Market	Potential customers may not perceive the need for product or service offered.	Market for proposed product or service may expand.
Project Objectives	Project objectives may not be a high priority to stakeholders.	Project objectives may inspire high-levels of sponsorship and commitment.
Portfolio Synergy	Project objectives may not be traceable to corporate vision and goals.	Project objectives may enhance overall corporate portfolio and goals.
Product or Service	Current markets for proposed product or service may be limited.	Current markets for proposed product or service may expand.
Results	Results may not be measurable.	Results may enhance overall corporate scorecard and goals.
Sponsorship	Adequate levels of sponsorship may be difficult to attain.	Optimal level of sponsorship may be attainable based on project objectives.
Technology	Proposed technological solution may not be accepted or supportable.	Proposed technical solution may enhance overall architectural stability and effectiveness.

Internal Business or Process Perspective Risks

Figure 5.3 lists some internal business or process perspective risks to consider. We again share common causes and events from both a negative risk and positive risk perspective. There are numerous impacts that stem from each potential event. This RBS is not meant to be all inclusive.

Figure 5.3 Internal Business or Process Perspective Risks

RBS: Internal Business or Process Perspective Risks		
Cause, Fact, Condition	**Potential Negative Events**	**Potential Positive Events**
Business Continuance/Disaster Recovery (BC/DR)	Solution may necessitate the need for redundant system back up in event of outages and downtime.	Solution may enhance current BC/DR environment, or alleviate current issues.
Communications	Cross-group collaboration may be impacted by multiple communications blockers.	Cross-group collaboration will likely be enhanced by well-developed network and channels.
Core Competencies	Solution may detract level of effort from organizational core workload.	Solution may enhance critical core competencies and competitive advantage.
Project Integration	Project may require extensive effort to integrate into current operational environment.	Project may easily integrate into current environment and enhance operations.
Quality	Solution may increase quality issues.	Solution may address and alleviate documented quality issues.
Resources	Solution may increase resources required to operate systems or execute processes.	Solution may reduce resources required to operate systems or execute processes.
Solution Fit	Solution may adversely impact current operations.	Solution may reduce issues with current operations.

RBS: Internal Business or Process Perspective Risks Continued		
Cause, Fact, Condition	Potential Negative Events	Potential Positive Events
Time	Solution has potential to increase time required to provide product or service.	Solution has potential to reduce time required to provide product or service.
Work Flow	May have dramatic negative effect on processes and workflow.	Potential to easily integrate new work into existing processes and workflow.

Employee or Innovation and Learning Perspective Risks

Figure 5.4 lists employee or innovation and learning perspective risks to consider. This RBS addresses potential risk events that may impact our most important resource—people.

Figure 5.4 Employee or Innovation and Learning Perspective Risks

RBS: Employee or Innovation and Learning Perspective Risks		
Cause, Fact, Condition	Potential Negative Events	Potential Positive Events
Adoption	Employees may resist implementation of new product or service.	Employees may embrace new product or service as highly beneficial.
Capacity	Employees may not have capacity to integrate new workload.	Employees may be able to seamlessly integrate new workload and succeed.
Change Management	Implementation of new product or service may catch employees by surprise.	Change management methodology may change resistance into support in rapid fashion.
Creativity	New product or service support may be perceived as non-value "busy work."	New product or service may inspire employee's creativity and innovation.
Motivation/Passion	Employees may not feel motivated to support project.	Product or service promise may motivate employees to passionately accept and support project.

RBS: Employee or Innovation and Learning Perspective Risks Continued		
Cause, Fact, Condition	**Potential Negative Events**	**Potential Positive Events**
Schedule Requirements	Schedule milestones may lead to conflict and delays.	Employee buy-in may lead to ability to accelerate schedule.
Team Mix	Team may not work well together due to past issues and conflicts.	Team may elevate to the high performance level rapidly.
Training	Extensive training requirements may result in schedule delays.	Well-defined training plan may lead to opportunities to roll out solution early.
Work Life Integration	Morale may suffer as a result of implementing this project.	Morale and productivity may increase as a result of implementing this project.

Customer Perspective Risks

Figure 5.5 lists some customer perspective risks to consider. This RBS looks at risk events that may impact, or be impacted by, our customer base.

Figure 5.5 Customer Perspective Risks

RBS: Customer Perspective Risks		
Cause, Fact, Condition	**Potential Negative Events**	**Potential Positive Events**
Adoption	Customers may resist implementation of new product or service.	Customers may embrace new product or service as value added.
Customer Satisfaction	Customer satisfaction may be negatively impacted.	Customer satisfaction may be positively impacted.
FURPS	Product or service offering may not satisfy customer expectations.	Product or service offering may meet and exceed customer expectations.

RBS: Customer Perspective Risks Continued		
Cause, Fact, Condition	**Potential Negative Events**	**Potential Positive Events**
Help Desk	Current staff may be unable to provide required levels of support.	Help desk staff may be able to integrate new product or service seamlessly.
Requirements	Pushing requirement at users may lead to resistance.	Customer will likely support 100% as project responds to their stated needs.
Service Level Agreements (SLA)	Project may negatively impact SLA requirements.	Project may enhance ability to meet and exceed SLA.
Support	Customers may deem support requirements as excessive.	Support requirements may be less than customer expectations.
Technology Maturity	Lack of customer understanding and appreciation of technology may lead to issues.	Customer understanding and appreciation of technology may lead to opportunities.

Planning Risk Responses

We provided an overview of potential risk causes and events in the previous section. It is important to show decision makers you understand potential risk causes and events that may impact the Business Case. This is an important step. However, there is an old business adage that states, "Never tell me there's a problem unless you have a solution." This holds true for risk events as well.

The likely question you will receive during your Business Case presentation is, "How do you plan to mitigate the risk?" You need to be able to respond with a solution that makes sense, and addresses the risk event adequately.

There are seven potential responses to risk. "Accept" is a response that addresses both positive and negative risks. We will define each potential response using language in the previously referenced *PMBOK ® Guide*. Understanding the seven different risk response options will allow you to address responses to the risk events you identify in your Business Case adequately.

Risk Responses for Negative Risk Events

There are four potential responses for negative risks. There may be times when you may use combinations of these response strategies to a single risk event.

1. **Avoid:** There are times when you can eliminate a cause for a negative risk. This is called an "Avoid" response. As an example, you may determine there is an adoption risk that may lead to employees resisting implementation of new product or service. The impact could be delays, failure to comply with new processes, frustration, and more. You may be able to avoid after-the-fact adoption risks by implementing effective change management to gain employee buy-in prior to the product or service launch. This response eliminates potential causes of a risk event.

2. **Transfer:** A "Transfer" response assigns accountability or responsibility of a potential risk event to a third-party. As an example, you are implementing a new process or system that requires support. Support of the new system is not a core competency in the organization. The risk event has the potential to require internal resources to apply their effort to support work that is not a core competency. The impact could be delays, resource shortages, frustration, etc. A transfer response brings in a third-party to accomplish the support workload that is not a core competency the organization needs to develop. A transfer response ensures support for the new system, and allows internal resources to focus on work supporting core processes.

3. **Mitigate:** A "Mitigate" response acknowledges that attempting to avoid the risk cause is not realistic or practical. Mitigating the risk aims to reduce the probability the risk event will occur, or reduce the negative impact of the risk event if it occurs. As an example, a Business Case proposes a technological solution that will automate a manual process. You sense resentment, frustration, and fear from the customer base. There is nothing you can do to address the cause. The automation program has to happen, and the technology is needed. However, you can reduce the probability of resentment, frustration, fear, and the potential negative impact that could follow, by implementing training to show the customers how the new system works, how to use it, key features that will help them perform, etc. Training is a common mitigate response.

4. **Accept:** There may be times when the best response to a risk is to allow it to occur and deal with the impact. You may choose to "Accept" a risk if you feel the impact is not critical, or easy to address. You may also accept a risk if there is no other response available. When you accept a risk, you do nothing to alter the cause, probability, or impact. An example could be a schedule risk. If there are delays, there will be frustration, conflict, and project constraint adjustments. There may be circumstances beyond your control that could lead to the schedule risk occurring. However, there is nothing more you can do from a proactive standpoint. You elect to manage the project as best you can, and address schedule slips if and when they occur. Note the accept response can be used for BOTH negative and positive risks!

Risk Responses for Positive Risk Events

There are four potential responses for positive risks as well. We discussed the "Accept" response strategy which also applies to positive risks. However, we will provide a positive risk example to revisit the accept response, along with explaining three new response strategies.

1. **Exploit:** The "Exploit" response method is the opposite of avoid. Develop an exploit response to try to enable a cause or situation that may lead to events with positive impacts you want to occur. As an example, you would like to be able to recommend a new system with all key components rather than a partial solution. You know that attaining funds is the key to success. The cause or situation revolves around attaining funding commitments. If you attain these commitments, multiple positive events and impacts will follow. Your response is to negotiate and gain funding commitment approval ahead of time to allow for the total system solution you desire.

2. **Share:** A "Share" response is the opposite of transfer. When you share, you bring in a third-party to help achieve an opportunity. As an example, you calculate costs of a key component to be $500 each. Your Business Case requires 50 of these components. You learn that another project manager needs the same component for her proposed solution. By coincidence, she needs 50 components as well. You learn that the company that provides the component gives volume discounts for orders of 100 components or more. You decide to partner with the other project manager to share the cost savings that result, and apply them to your Business Case.

3. **Enhance:** An "Enhance" response is the opposite of mitigate. Develop an enhance response to increase the probability and/or impact of a positive risk event occurring. As an example, you are proposing a solution in a Business Case that will allow your organization to meet a Service Level Agreement (SLA) that calls for 90% system reliability. There is an automation feature that may increase reliability to near 95%. You decide to enhance probability that the automation feature will work by developing a prototype to test the impact before you move forward with your recommendation.

4. **Accept:** We discussed "Accept" as a response to negative risk events. It also applies to positive risk events. As an example, you are proposing a process improvement project with the potential to improve morale and overall Work Life Integration for the organization's employees. You decide to concentrate on improving the process and making it work. You will be pleased if morale is positively impacted, but elect to take no definitive action outside of being aware of the probability.

Documenting Risks: Risk Register

Your next job in the Risk Management Process is to document your risks. A best practice in risk management to document applicable risks and responses is called a *Risk Register.* A Risk Register should be part of every Business Case.

Figure 5.6 shows an example of a sample Risk Register with two contrasting entries. One example is a negative risk or threat. The other example is a positive risk or opportunity. Remember, there are two types of risk!

We will review basic Risk Register components. Feel free to add additional columns or information you may feel is pertinent to your specific Business Case. Common additions include risk event and impact costs, benefits, resource requirements, etc.

Figure 5.6 Risk Register Example

Risk Cause and Event	Impact	Probability Risk Rating	Impact Risk Rating	Risk Score	Triggers/Response
Cause: Help Desk Skill Level Deficiencies. **Negative Risk Event:** Help Desk may not be able to address questions on the new proposed technology.	Customer complaints will increase. CSAT will drop.	4	5	20	**Trigger:** Increased issues and complaints. **Response:** Initiate training on new system support. Develop FAC reference for Help Desk use.
Cause: Technology Enhancement. **Positive Risk Event:** Proposed solution may address current technology issues.	Complaints and delays may be reduced.	3	3	9	**Response:** Consider incentives to expedite system implementation.

- **Cause:** Define the cause that may lead to the risk event. Note: Some Risk Registers add a stand-alone "Cause" column.

- **Risk Event:** Define the potential risk event in plain terms. Be accurate, brief, and concise. Note that a Risk Register can be used to document both negative and positive risks. Most managers normally develop a method to segregate the two types of risks, rather than group them together as a single list. For example, you may want to break out your Risk Register into Part I: Negative Risks, and Part II: Positive Risks.

- **Impact:** Describe the impact if the risk event occurs. In the Help Desk example, the impact is negative. In the Technology risk example, the impact is positive.

- **Probability Risk Rating:** Develop a numeric method to determine the probability of the risk event occurring. A simple scale is 1 – 5. You may elect to use a different scale such as 1 – 7. That is fine. Just rate all risks consistently using the same rating system. Here is an example of a sample Probability Risk Rating scale.

  o **Probability 1:** Low (0% - 20%)

  o **Probability 2:** Low to Moderate (21% - 40%)

  o **Probability 3:** Moderate (41% - 60%)

  o **Probability 4:** Moderate to High (61% - 80%)

  o **Probability 5:** High (81% - 99%)

- **Impact Risk Rating:** Impact is a measure of how the risk event will impact your proposed solution either negatively or positively. An example of a simple scale you can use is the 1-3-5 scale as shown below. Again, alternative scales are acceptable.

  o **Impact Level 1:** Low Impact: For a negative risk, easy workaround and minimum impact on scope, schedule, cost, and quality. For a positive risk, a "nice to have."

  o **Impact Level 3:** Moderate Impact: For a negative risk, impact will require a moderate level of effort to address. Potential to negatively impact key objectives is high. For a positive risk, this is a "should have."

  o **Impact Level 5:** High Impact: For a negative risk, this will require a high-level of effort to address. Key objectives will be impacted dramatically. Expect a combination of schedule slips, cost overruns, quality issues, and potential scope issues. For a positive risk, this is a "must have."

- **Risk Score:** A Risk Score is calculated by multiplying the Probability Risk Rating times the Impact Risk Rating. Refer to the Help Desk example. A Probability Risk Rating of 4 times an Impact Risk Rating of 5 equals 20. We would prioritize the Help Desk risk higher than the Technology risk which has a Risk Score of 9. This method of determining a Risk Score is referred to as *Qualitative Risk Analysis.*

- **Triggers:** There may be times when you can predict the occurrence of a risk event before it occurs. For example, ominous clouds, thunder, and lightning often give us an early warning before a storm occurs. These early warning events are referred to as *triggers*. Adding triggers in your response when applicable is a best practice. It eases the fears that a risk may undo all the good your Business Case will accomplish. Trigger events prompt you to implement your response early. Note that many risk events may not have a trigger.

- **Response:** Your response should directly address the risk event, impact, and be tailored to the Risk Score. High priority risks with a high Risk Score generally require a more aggressive response than lower priority risks. We provide some general response strategies that impact multiple risk causes and events in our final "Summary and Tips" section.

Defining Risk: Summary and Tips

This brings us to the end of the Define Risk chapter. Here is a quick summary of what we covered, and the key points you need to take away.

- **Risk Defined:** Risk is an uncertain event that has not yet occurred. There are negative risks which can lead to threats. There are positive risks that can lead to opportunities. Try to identify both types. It is best to identify as many potential risks as possible. Known risks can be dealt with. Unknown risks are the most dangerous, and will find you at the most inopportune time.

- **Risk Meta-Language:** Every risk has three components. Remember the cause-event-impact definition methodology. The first component is the cause of the risk. This can be a cause, situation, fact, or condition. Each cause may result in events occurring that are both positive and negative. A single cause can result in multiple events. Each event has potential positive and/or negative impacts. Keep this relationship in mind when defining risks and developing tailored responses.

- **Risk Responses:** The mitigate response is everyone's favorite. However, there are seven other response options if you count the "Accept" response twice. Evaluate each risk and apply the most appropriate response type to address the risk.

o There may be times when you use multiple response methods to respond to risk. As an example, you could have a technology risk for a new unproven system you are proposing. You may elect a multi-faceted response strategy. Begin with a mitigate approach by training new personnel on the system. Then follow up the mitigate response with an enhance response. Offer incentives to roll out the new system ahead of schedule.

o Always consider the risk adversity or *risk utility* of your stakeholders. How high or low are there risk tolerances. If you know that budget is not a key issue, don't spend time prioritizing budget risks high, developing responses, and sharing with key decision makers. On the other hand, if decision makers have low tolerance, definitely address these risks.

o There are a number of common response strategies that apply to multiple risk causes and events. These common "fixes" include, but are not limited to:

- **ABC:** Accuracy, brevity, and clarity/conciseness are three traits that eliminate many potential risk causes and events. Ambiguity is not a Business Case developer's friend.

- **Assumptions:** Assumptions are defined as facts we believe to be true, but have yet to validate. You need to validate all assumptions. Each assumption is a risk waiting to happen.

- **Communications:** The Project Management Institute (PMI) states that a successful manager spends approximately 90% of his or her time communicating. Effective communication can address multiple risk causes and events.

- **Change Management:** We cover effective change management more in the next chapter. Many great ideas encounter resistance, and ultimately fail to achieve objectives due to adoption issues. Always prepare stakeholders for change.

- **Stakeholder Management:** A stakeholder is anyone with an interest in, or potentially impacted by, a project proposal. Providing stakeholders with the right information at the right time helps avoid and mitigate numerous risks. We discuss this critical area more in the next chapter as well.

- **Audience Adaptability:** Different stakeholders have different views. Some embrace certain objectives or value propositions over others. Know your audience, and develop and present your Business Case in a way that satisfies the audience's needs. We discuss this concept at much greater length in later chapters.

- **Risk Register:** Document risks and proposed responses in a Risk Register. The Risk Register should be part of your overall Business Case, and be made available for decision makers to review.

  - **Probability Risk Rating:** Assign Probability Risk Ratings to each risk using a standardized approach. Risk is an event that has the potential to occur. Different risks have differing probabilities of occurring.

  - **Impact Risk Rating:** Some risks have more impact than others. Assign Impact Risk Ratings using a standardized approach.

  - **Risk Score:** Risk Score is calculated by multiplying the Probability Risk Rating probability times the Impact Risk Rating. Spend more time developing responses on risks that score the highest. Place low scoring risks on a *"Watch List."* Keep an eye on these risks, but don't devote a lot of time or energy on risk responses unless the Risk Score moves upward.

  - **Secondary Risks:** Be aware of *Secondary Risks*. These are risks that may occur as a result of a risk response. For example, you elect to mitigate a risk by developing a training program. The secondary risk is that the training program may not adequately upgrade skills as desired.

o **Residual Risks:** Be aware of *Residual Risks* as well. Residual Risks are defined as potential risk impacts that remain after a primary risk response is implemented. For example, a risk response may address 80% of the impacts of a risk event. The Residual Risk is the 20% that remains. A city may choose to apply salt to roads in the event of a snow storm as their primary risk response. The Residual Risk would be the impact of the salt on the roads after the storm subsides. You may need a secondary response to deal with the impact of the salt. Residual Risks should be addressed on a Risk Register when known. As a rule of thumb, the negative impact of a Residual Risk should never be greater than the negative impact of the primary risk event. If this is the case, it is highly recommended that you rethink your primary risk response strategy.

You are almost finished with the development phase of the Business Case. A blank Risk Register is provided as "Food For Thought" on the next page.

Review and use the Risk Register. Then get ready to learn about additional information you may need to address and provide in your Business Case. Chapter 6 addresses additional considerations that may spell the difference between success and failure!

Chapter 5 "Food For Thought"

Brainstorm potential risks that may impact your Business Case. Complete the blank Risk Register below. Negative risks are easy to identify. Try to identify a positive risk or two as well.

Risk Cause and Event	Impact	Probability Risk Rating	Impact Risk Rating	Risk Score	Triggers/Response

My Notes:

Chapter 6: Provide Supporting Data and Information

We discussed the need to clearly define objectives and develop a viable value proposition for your Business Case. We defined and illustrated key financials you will likely be expected to provide, and explored risks that can potentially enhance, or negatively impact, the value you shared. To this point, we have discussed what, why, how much, and what if factors.

There are a number of additional considerations that may be applicable to your Business Case. This chapter outlines supporting data that may be required to gain approval of your proposal. These include how, who, and when factors.

Change Management Considerations

Stakeholders are often very reluctant to accept and embrace change. This reluctance can lead to resistance, which could lead to adoption risks materializing that jeopardize the project you are proposing. Figure 6.1 provides an overview of the Lewin Change Model. We can use this model as a guide to determine steps you may need to include in your Business Case to define a change management methodology.

Figure 6.1 Lewin Change Model

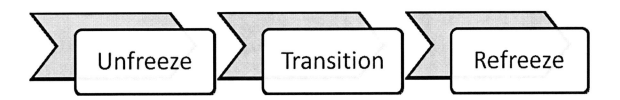

You will likely be asked to describe your plan to integrate the new product or service you propose into the workforce. The Lewin Change Model provides a three-step process that has proven successful in managing change. Let's review the three steps.

1. **Unfreeze:** You need to reach out to all impacted stakeholders and provide a value proposition that motivates them to accept your proposal. If your solution has potential to improve the organization's financial perspective, process perspective, employee perspective, or customer perspective; share the good news in a manner that satisfies each stakeholder group's "WII-FM" criteria.

   - WII-FM stands for "What's in it for me." The WII-FM factor for internal employees may differ from that of customers. The finance team may very well have a totally different interpretation of value as compared to the operations team. Match the WII-FM to the individual stakeholder group, and prepare them to accept change accordingly.

   - If your proposal has negative repercussions such as employee downsizing, benefits decreases, etc., make sure you share the business imperative for implementing the Business Case proposal. Stakeholders will not "jump for joy." However, resistance will be reduced through understanding, honesty, and open communications.

2. **Transition:** The second step of the Lewin Change Model is the transition phase. Once you unfreeze stakeholders, and they become receptive to change, lead them through the change process and make it easy for them. Your Business Case should contain a high-level strategy to include stakeholders in the change process. Keys to success are effective communications, responding to questions, managing issues, and sharing wins as each phase unfolds. Rewarding people for their efforts is a great best practice that accelerates the transition phase.

3. **Refreeze:** There is potential for stakeholders to slip back to the prior way of doing business. To avoid this risk, you need to counter this potential. When the project goal is met, thank all stakeholders for their contribution. Advertise the win and give credit where credit is due. Ensure all stakeholders receive adequate training ahead of time, and answer questions as they occur. Consider incentives for stakeholders who integrate the new change into operations. Sustain the gain!

The Stakeholder Register

Many projects fail when affected stakeholders are not identified early in the Business Case process, and effectively communicated with. It is important to identify stakeholders, and explain their roles up-front during the Business Case development phase. This action allows you and stakeholders to share mutual expectations, partner to achieve success, and mitigate a number of potential stakeholder generated risks.

Figure 6.2 provides a Stakeholder Register that applies a "RACI" methodology. The RACI acronym stands for "Responsible, Accountable, Consult, and Inform."

Figure 6.2 Stakeholder Register

Stakeholder	Organization	Role	R	A	C	I	Comments
Bob Winkler	ABC Business	Proposed Sponsor	X	X		X	Meet on Oct 25th to discuss Business Case. Assignment pending.
Mary Smith	Operations	Support Liaison	X		X		Shared potential capacity and funding issues. Listed as risks. Meet in 2 weeks.
Rob Childress	PMO	Project Manager (PM)	X	X			PMO assigns Rob as the PM when the Business Case is approved.

A Stakeholder Register should define basic information about the stakeholder, their organization, and their role in the proposed project. At minimum, include:

1. **Stakeholder Identification and Organization:** Document applicable stakeholder by name or position. Identify and document their organization.

2. **Role:** Document role the Stakeholder will serve. RACI is an appropriate tool. Each stakeholder is assigned one or more roles. For example, Mary is assigned Responsible and Consult roles. Bob, on the other hand, is assigned Responsible, Accountable, and Inform roles.

3. **Specific Roles (RACI):**

- **R: Responsible:** Stakeholder will be required to accomplish work activities.

- **A: Accountable:** Stakeholder assumes management responsibility for the project. Stakeholder is accountable for key deliverables or results.

- **C: Consult:** Provides advice, guidance, and expertise. Stakeholder fulfills role of Subject Matter Expert (SME).

- **I: Inform:** Stakeholder is kept informed of project status, issues, etc. Status may change as the project moves forward.

4. **Comments:** Include specific comments regarding stakeholder inputs, roles, issues, etc. This could include meetings, next steps, clarifying notes, etc.

Schedule Considerations

Your Business Case should provide a high-level Work Breakdown Structure (WBS) and schedule to answer the "When and How" questions you will likely need to respond to. Most Business Cases propose a solution that will be implemented as a project. The three key considerations for every project are time, cost, and scope. This section addresses the time component.

A WBS is an overview of all project work activities. A high-level WBS is a great tool you can use to address project "When" and "How" questions during the Business Case presentation if asked.

Figure 6.3 is a high-level WBS organized in the proven format of "PDCA." The PDCA acronym stands for Plan-Do-Check-Act, and is a foundational concept used in project management. The first step in project management is to make a *"Plan."* The second step is to *"Do"* what is in the project plan. *"Check"* to make sure you accomplish what is defined in the plan. Finally, *"Act"* accordingly based on your check. If everything is accomplished according to the plan, move forward. If there are issues, address them. We will use this method to model a Work Breakdown Structure technique you may wish to employ.

Figure 6.3 Work Breakdown Structure (WBS) Example

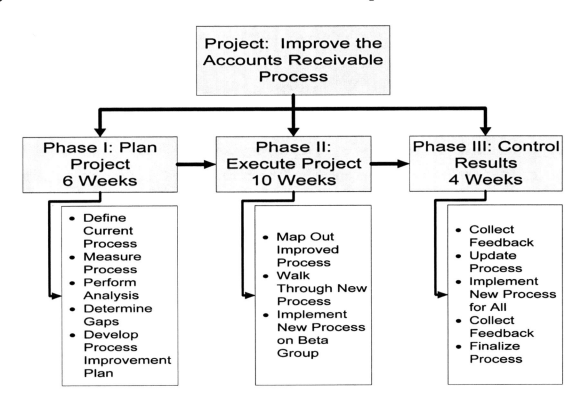

Figure 6.3 is a sample WBS that shows the high-level plan to improve an accounts receivable process. Key components of the WBS include:

- **A high-level overview of the project**: Level 1 is the project objective. In this case, we propose a project to "Improve the Accounts Receivable Process."

- **A level 2 breakout**: Level 2 activities are the individual steps or phases in the project. Breaking out the project into phases satisfies three key objectives:

1. A phased approach shows decision makers you have a plan or vision of how the project will be executed end-to-end. Project phasing addresses preliminary "How" questions.

2. A phased approach gives decision makers choices. Your preferred approach may be to accomplish all three phases in a single project. Decision makers may be reluctant to commit to the entire project. However, they may be open to committing to a phased approach. They may approve completion of Phase I. They will then issue a Go/No-Go decision to proceed to Phase II.

3. A phased approach allows you to provide approximate time frames required to complete each phase. This answers "When" questions. In the example, the total time requirement to complete the project is 6 + 10 + 4 = 20 weeks.

- **A high-level description of work activities to be accomplished:** It is beneficial to provide a brief outline of proposed work activities to be accomplished in each phase. PDCA works well! This gives decision makers the opportunity to review your high-level plan, and provide input as necessary. More importantly, it shows you know what you are doing! Credibility is a key Critical Success Factor you need to establish.

Legal/Compliance Considerations

Ensure your proposal considers both legal and compliance factors. Legal considerations may include factors as licenses, permits, laws, etc. Regulatory factors dictated by the government also must be considered.

Compliance factors may include considerations such as Occupational Safety and Health Administration rules (OSHA), Sarbanes-Oxley (SOX) compliance, International Organization for Standardization (ISO) certification compliance, etc.

Legal and compliance considerations can also address constraints. These are boundaries we must stay within as dictated by many possible directives, regulations, policies, procedures, etc.

Architectural Impact

Make note of the current organizational environment. What systems are in place? What are current organizational plans to modify and improve current systems? What new core competencies are needed, and which are being de-emphasized? You want to ensure your Business Case proposal is synergistic with the existing and planned environment whenever possible.

There may be times when your Business Case proposes a solution that is contrary to the existing architectural environment. If this is the case, your argument for change will need to be extremely convincing to gain approval. This does not mean you should not pursue change that is beneficial. It does mean that your battle to gain approval will likely be more challenging.

Post Implementation Tracking Plan

Many decision makers want to know your plan to track your value proposition to see if the promise made in the Business Case truly becomes a reality after the project is implemented. Having a Post Implementation Tracking Plan in your Business Case increases the credibility and viability of your proposal, and often leads to more favorable consideration and approval.

Figure 6.4 provides an overview of some of the most common value propositions offered in Business Cases, and guidance on how to track the benefits. This list maps to the Balanced Scorecard model introduced earlier. We have four tables for your review broken out by Balanced Scorecard perspectives as follows:

- 6.4.1: **Financial Perspective**

- 6.4.2: **Internal or Business Process Perspective**

- 6.4.3: **Employee or Innovation and Learning Perspective**

- 6.4.4: **Customer Perspective**

Figure 6.4 Post Implementation Tracking Plan Considerations

6.4.1 Financial Perspective

Perspective	Value Proposition	Tracking Considerations
Financial	**Compliance/ Regulatory/ Legal**	• Documentation or validation that your solution conforms to requirements.
	Cost Avoidance	• Documented data showing the costs that will be reduced, and a timeframe for the costs to be eliminated from the budget.
	Cost Savings	• A time-phased overview of applicable cost savings, and the timeframe they can be removed from the budget. • *Note: Most cost savings don't actually materialize until the project is underway. Be realistic!*
	EPS/Revenue	• Marketing research data that substantiates claims. • Testimonials/requirements from customers. Time-phased revenue projections.
	Effectiveness	• Testimonials/requirements from customers. • Reduced complaints or revenue projections.
	Risk Reduction	• Before and after Risk Register that compares Risk Scores and the number of risks before and after the proposed project is implemented. • Reduced overall Risk Score for threats, and increased overall Risk Score for opportunities.
	Portfolio Support	• Documentation that proves traceability of your project to the overall organizational portfolio. Proof of synergy.
	Satisfy Shareholders	• Provide quantifiable information in form of surveys that solution is favorable to stakeholders. • Track solution back to complaints and develop timetable to measure reduction of negative issues. • Provide plan to measure before and after CSAT or NSAT scores.

Tracking financial benefits and fulfilling the promises made in the Business Case add credibility to you and your team. It also paves the way for future Business Case approvals as well. Decision makers love to support a winner!

As we shared previously, cost savings and revenue benefits take time to materialize. A huge mistake is forecasting benefits from day one of the project. Try to forecast a reasonable time phase when benefits will be realized. Don't set false expectations, or make promises your project may not be able to keep!

6.4.2 Internal Business or Process Perspective

Perspective	Value Proposition	Tracking Considerations
Internal Business or Process	**Competitive Advantage**	• Compare the FURPS criteria for your product versus the competitor's. Do you win? • Provide a before and after overview of your product—show what will be gained. • Point to data sources that confirm you listened to the Voice of the Customer. Testimonials are huge!
	Core Competencies	• Show data that quantifies core competency issues and solutions you provided. • Validate correction of issues with key stakeholders—provide support. • Measure improvement after the project is complete through interviews, observation, productivity metrics, etc.
	Efficiency	• See the time and resource reduction sections on the next page. Efficiency is measured in terms of faster time and fewer resources.
	Improve Quality	• Track costs of failure: Reduction of reworks, scrap, returns, etc. • Track costs of non-conformance: Reduction in liabilities, warranty work, lost business, etc.
	Process Mapping and Improvement	• Develop process maps—show prior gaps, issues, and inefficiencies. • Show "As Is" versus "To Be" process maps. Show how efficiencies were achieved. • Measure "To Be" results. Provide feedback.

Perspective	Value Proposition	Tracking Considerations
Internal Business or Process Continued	**Process Time Reductions**	• Measure time required for the current or "As Is" process. • Forecast time reductions and track the "To Be" process to determine actual results. Share feedback.
	Process Resource Reductions	• Measure resources required to support the "As Is" process. Resources are personnel costs for internal and external resources, equipment, supply, and material costs. • Forecast resource cost reductions and track "To Be" savings to determine actual results. Share feedback.
	SLA	• Determine current SLA criteria. Measure "As Is" results. • Measure "To Be" results. Compare. Provide feedback.

Many companies are relatively effective. They provide a great product or service that the customer values. Oftentimes, these same companies are quite inefficient. It costs far more time and resources to get to the desired output than it should.

It is worth reiterating a key point. Profitability is impacted in two ways. First, you can sell more of your product to increase sales and revenue. We addressed this consideration in the financial perspective section. Secondly, you can reduce the costs required to make your products or services. Providing products and services faster and reducing resource costs is the essence of the internal business or process perspective.

6.4.3 Employee or Innovation and Learning Perspective

Perspective	Value Proposition	Tracking Considerations
Employee or Innovation and Learning	Adoption	• Survey stakeholders before, during, and after the project. Determine what is going well, what can be improved, and make applicable changes.
	Creativity and Leverage Skills	• Survey employees. Determine if employees feel they can more creatively use their skills as a result of the improved product or service. • Solicit feedback and plan next steps.
	Morale and Passion, Teamwork, Work Life Integration	• Measure levels of employee satisfaction before and after. Report results. • Measure staff turnover, absenteeism, complaints, etc. • Plan next steps. Take action.
	Training	• **Survey employees:** "Did this training help you perform at a higher level?" • **Observation:** Is there less confusion, fewer questions, etc.? • **Requests for Clarification:** Have verbal, e-mail, etc. requests for clarification been reduced? • **Productivity:** Has time to implement been reduced? Is resource consumption reduced? • **Dependence:** Is dependence on alternate internal sources or external vendors reduced?

Andrew Carnegie was an industrialist and philanthropist who lived in the 1800's. He once stated that a firm could have all the money in the world, magnificent buildings, and superb products. However, "without the right people, nothing else really matters." Andrew Carnegie's words are still true today. People add value.

6.4.4 Customer Perspective

Perspective	Value Proposition	Tracking Considerations
Customer	Complaints Management	• Log/track complaints prior to implementation of the proposed solution. • Log/track complaints after implementation of the proposed solution. Look for reduction in numbers.
	CSAT	• Measure customer satisfaction on a 1-5 or similar scale. Measure before and after project completion. • Track changes. If project was successful, CSAT should increase.
	Customer Partnership Experience	• Track number of service requests. Track and share upward or downward trends. • Track returns, complaints, lost customers, etc. Track and share upward and downward trends.
	NSAT	• Survey customers asking if they are very satisfied, satisfied, neutral, somewhat dissatisfied, or very dissatisfied with the effectiveness of your product or service. • Strive for more very satisfied responses. Strive to reduce somewhat dissatisfied and very dissatisfied responses. • *Note: NSAT formula:* (Number of Very Satisfied Responses / Total Number of Survey Responses) – (Number of Somewhat Dissatisfied Responses + Number of Very Dissatisfied Responses). The higher the score, the better!
	Voice of the Customer (VOC)	• Reach out to customers for input. Track responses. • Show how your project addresses customer needs. • Share customer feedback and results.

I will caveat on the Andrew Carnegie quote shared earlier. You can have a great financial plan, processes, and even motivated employees. However, if you have no customers—you are in big trouble. Customers buy products and services, and keep organizations and companies in business. Track metrics that reflect customer perceptions, opinions, and actions. These are metrics that matter!

Required Sponsorship

You need to determine who is best positioned to sponsor your Business Case. There are two considerations that will lead to success or failure in achieving appropriate sponsorship. The first consideration is your Business Case itself. Follow the guidance we have provided. Build a solid Business Case.

The second consideration is your presentation. You need to make a positive impression. We will discuss this important piece of the equation in subsequent chapters.

We covered a number of essential steps you need to consider when building a Business Case. Here is a brief summary of guidance and tips we have shared up to this point:

- **Objectives:** Make sure your objectives are clear and understandable. Avoid ambiguity and concentrate on stating "What" you propose. Remember the action-result methodology.

- **Value Proposition:** Understand the sponsor's "Why" perspective. Frame your value proposition in a way that is meaningful to the sponsor you are seeking.

- **Costs and Benefits:** Seek a level of sponsorship that is appropriate to the overall cost of your proposal. Ensure all cost and benefit data is accurate and supportable. Have a plan in place to track benefits after the project is complete.

- **Risk:** Try to determine which risks are obvious that the sponsor may be aware of. Use a Risk Register to address those risks, and define responses, on a situational basis.

- **Other Information:** Try to anticipate additional information the sponsor may desire and include it in your Business Case. In addition, try to gain a level of sponsorship that is at a higher level than key stakeholders with the power to impact your proposal. The right sponsor can intervene as necessary to ensure the approved project stays on-track.

- **Options Rule of 3:** Try to offer three options in your Business Case. Include "As Is" as an option. Remember that the "As Is" option may be your preferred option.

    o Some Business Cases define a total end-to-end solution, and a phased solution. Your recommendation is your preferred option.

    o Other Business Cases offer non-related options. When this is the case, share the two most likely options, your recommendation, and include an "As Is" option.

    o You may solicit solutions from stakeholders and receive multiple of options. Choose the two most feasible along with the "As Is" option. Provide a list of options not considered with rationale in the Appendix of the Business Case.

Figure 6.5 provides a scoring tool you may wish to use if you have multiple options you need to choose from.

Figure 6.5 Business Case Option Scoring Matrix

Business Case Option Scoring Matrix Directions: Score #1 Choice as a (1). Score #2 Choice as a (2), etc. Low score is the preferred choice.						
Options	**Stakeholder A Ranking**	**Stakeholder B Ranking**	**Stakeholder C Ranking**	**Stakeholder D Ranking**	**Stakeholder E Ranking**	**TOTAL**
Option A	3	2	3	1	4	13
Option B	2	1	4	3	2	12
Option C	1	3	1	2	1	8
Option D	4	4	2	4	3	17

In this example, there are four options and five stakeholders. Each stakeholder ranks their preferred options from 1 to 4. A 1 score reflects the stakeholder's highest choice. A 4 score reflects the lowest choice (See directions on the matrix).

- Option C is the recommended option. It has the lowest total by far.

We completed our discussion of how to prepare a solid Business Case. Chapter 7 shares some key tools and techniques you may find valuable. After this discussion, we explore the all-important presentation piece to ensure your Business Case is a winner!

Chapter 6 "Food For Thought"

Use the checklist below to determine which supporting data and information is pertinent to your Business Case. If there is a yes answer, make a comment and add it to your Business Case.

Question	Yes or No	Comments
Do I need a change management plan?		
Is a Stakeholder Register needed to identify and manage stakeholders?		
Are there enough stakeholders with diverse roles to warrant a RACI?		
Do I need a high-level schedule to present to decision makers?		
Are there legal, and/or compliance considerations I need to address?		
Are pertinent architectural impacts a consideration?		
Is a post implementation tracking methodology required?		
Do I need to address specific sponsorship requirements?		

My Notes:

Chapter 7: Business Case Tools and Techniques

There are a number of tools and techniques that are available which may help you in developing your Business Case. This chapter introduces some common, and not so common, tools and techniques you may wish to consider.

Group Creativity Techniques

There are a number of tools and techniques designed to tap into a group's creative minds and extract the information you need. These tools and techniques are categorized as *Group Creativity Techniques*. The following provides a definition and the applicability of four of the most common techniques.

Brainstorming

Brainstorming is a method that a Business Case developer may use to solicit objectives, value propositions, costs and benefits, risks, and more. Here is a quick overview of the goals, methods, dos, and don'ts of Brainstorming.

- **Goal:** Document as many thoughts and ideas as possible. The more ideas that are shared, the more successful the Brainstorming session.

- **Method:** Here is a step by step approach.

  1. A facilitator meets with a group of stakeholders with knowledge on a particular subject. Brainstorming sessions are best conducted face-to-face. However, live meeting, teleconferencing, etc. are other options.

  2. The facilitator states the objective or purpose. These are the only boundaries imposed. Be as clear as possible about the information required from the Brainstorming session. Set a goal everyone understands.

3. The facilitator solicits inputs. The facilitator may choose to use sticky notes initially to gather ideas. Or, the facilitator may share the objective, and write quickly as responses are shared. Beginning with sticky notes, and then opening up the session to verbal inputs, normally works best. It allows everyone to contribute, and mitigates the risk of one or two individuals in the group providing the majority of ideas or input.

- **Tips:** Do not evaluate ideas during a Brainstorming session. If you do so, it will slow down idea generation, and may intimidate members into becoming silent. Avoid hostility, and set a ground rule up-front that all ideas are welcomed. No idea is out of bounds. Finally, watch the non-verbal signals you share. Try to avoid non-verbal signals that reflect disagreement with ideas.

Nominal Group Technique

Nominal Group Technique is a method that a Business Case developer may use to solicit objectives, value propositions, costs and benefits, risks, and more. Nominal Group Technique is similar to Brainstorming with an added feature. Here is a quick overview of the goals, methods, dos, and don'ts.

- **Goal:** Evaluate the ideas received during a Brainstorming session and prioritize them by rank ordering each idea in terms of criticality or importance.

- **Method:** Here is a step by step approach.

1. A facilitator meets with a group of stakeholders with knowledge on a particular subject. The facilitator provides a list of ideas to the group. You may begin with a Brainstorming session, or may conduct a Nominal Group Technique meeting as a stand-alone session.

2. The facilitator asks participants to rank order each idea based on defined criteria. You could use clarifiers of importance, criticality to the customer, costs, benefits, etc. Sticky notes work best for this part of the meet. You want to gain an idea of the total group's prioritization. If you try to rank through discussion, a few individuals may use the forum as a platform to express their opinions and try to sway others.

3. Collect the ranking inputs. Determine how many choices you will rank. Complete a quick list with the overall rankings. You may only be concerned about the top 3 choices. Others may be concerned with the top 5, etc. Reiterate the rank order objectives, and share the results with the group.

4. Make time for everyone to share their opinions on the rank-ordered list. This is the participant's chance to share their thoughts on why the rankings should be accepted, or be reconsidered.

5. Ask the participants to once again rank order each option using sticky notes. Share the final result. Gain consensus as much as possible.

- **Tips:** Try to gain everyone's input. Expect some individuals to try to dominate the meeting. Use of solid facilitation techniques will win the day. Expect some individuals to disagree with the final rank order. Express understanding of their feelings. However, do your best to gain everyone's acceptance based on the needs and wants of the group as a whole.

Delphi Technique

Delphi Technique is a method used to gather information from experts in a way that reduces fear on the part of the participants. The key to a successful Delphi Technique exercise is assuring each participant that their specific input will remain anonymous and not be shared. Delphi Technique is a great method to use when defining objectives, value propositions, costs and benefits, risks, etc.

- **Goal:** Gain input from experts in a manner that ensures confidentiality. Analyze the inputs, and share overall findings with the experts who provided the input and other key stakeholders. Again, do not share individual inputs.

- **Method:** Here is a step by step approach.

  1. Determine experts who you want to solicit input from. Develop a survey or questionnaire and send it to each expert.

  2. Gather responses and consolidate findings. Do not attribute any input to the expert who provided it.

  3. Provide consolidated findings or results to key stakeholders to include the experts who provided the input for the final report. Take appropriate follow-on actions as necessary.

- **Tips:** Ensure all contributors understand you will treat inputs as confidential. You may have to establish some initial trust with the experts to win them over. Expect some pressure to reveal your sources. You will need to resist that pressure to maintain trust and integrity.

Mind Mapping/Affinity Charting

Mind mapping is a creativity technique you perform alone. You begin with an objective and start mentally Brainstorming. You record your ideas, and categorize them into a visual map. You use the map as a source to generate new ideas. Affinity charting is the same as mind mapping with one difference. Affinity charting is mind mapping facilitated in a group environment.

- **Goal:** Identify ideas and information pertinent to your subject. Place information and ideas into categories and sub-categories. Affinity charting is a great tool and technique your team can use to Brainstorm key information needed to develop a successful Business Case.

- **Method:** Here is a step by step approach.

    1. Define the Objective. Ensure you include stakeholders who have knowledge of the objective and can provide valued input.

    2. Find a whiteboard, flipchart, or table. Draw a circle and define your objective.

    3. Pass out sticky notes. Ask stakeholders to write down information pertinent to the objective. There are no boundaries imposed.

    4. Collect sticky notes and begin categorizing. See Figure 7.1 for an example of an affinity chart pertinent to our objective of developing a winning Business Case.

Figure 7.1 Affinity Chart Example

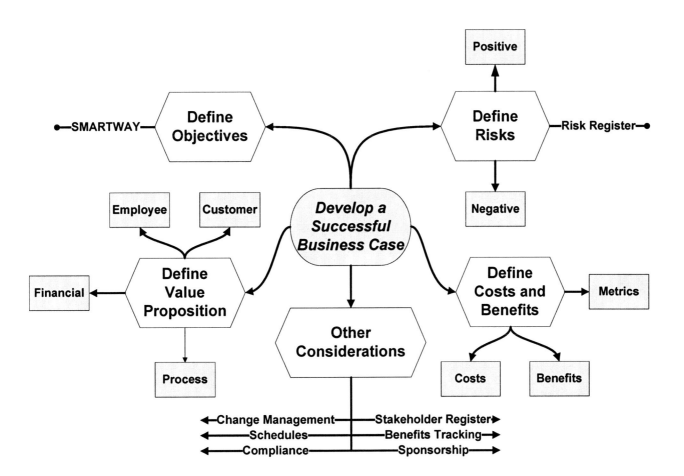

- **Tips:** Use a variety of shapes and lines to construct your mind map/affinity chart. There are a number of software applications available to help you develop your final product. Figure 7.1 was created using shapes in Microsoft Visio. There are multiple iterations of shapes, formats, etc. for affinity charts. Select the tool and technique that works best for you and your team.

SWOT Analysis (Strengths, Weaknesses, Opportunities, Threats)

SWOT is a tool that can help you identify objectives, applicable value propositions, benefits, and risks. SWOT stands for "Strengths, Weaknesses, Opportunities, and Threats." Figure 7.2 provides a visual overview of SWOT categories and considerations.

Figure 7.2 SWOT Categories and Considerations

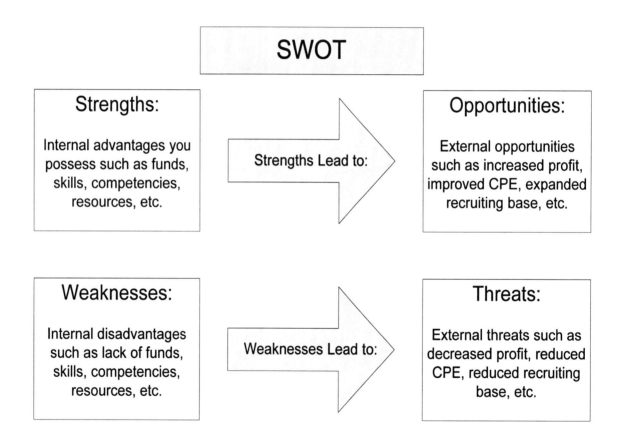

SWOT is a foundational tool used to develop "The Business Case for Life Decisions" we will discuss at length in Chapter 11. It is also a very applicable tool to help develop a traditional Business Case as well. Here is a breakout of how you can use SWOT to your advantage.

- **Defining Objectives:** SWOT provides guidance on how to develop solid objectives that have meaning to decision makers. SWOT can be used to gauge the health and welfare of the organization.

  - **Identify needed strengths and opportunities:** Some organizations have strengths that are underutilized. A Business Case could propose a plan to create needed strengths. A solid objective can also revolve around strengths you possess that could lead to achieving opportunities. For example, you may have additional funds left over from a prior project. Use that financial strength to capture a potential opportunity.

  - **Eliminate or reduce weaknesses or threats:** Some organizations may have weaknesses. Weaknesses often lead to threats. A solid objective you might propose is an idea to reduce a weakness which will lead to threats. For example, a lack of skill sets could lead to the threat of poor products and lost business. You might address this weakness by proposing a skill-based training program.

- **Defining the Value Proposition:** Analyzing an organization from a SWOT standpoint provides a snapshot of how the organization is poised to take advantage of opportunities, or be negatively impacted by threats. Perform a quick SWOT Analysis and use the following guidance as potential value propositions you can leverage in your Business Case.

  - **Increase strengths:** Some Business Cases can move the organization from "good to great." Use these impacts to your advantage.

  - **Position strengths to attain opportunities:** Review potential opportunities to be gained by increasing strengths. Build your Business Case around achievement of an opportunity that will be valued by decision makers.

o **Eliminate weaknesses that lead to threats:** Gain consensus that the weaknesses and threats you identify have high impact. Use this consensus as the basis for developing your Business Case objectives.

- **Risk Identification:** SWOT Analysis is a primary tool used by risk managers to identify and qualify risk.

  o Strengths lead to opportunities. A SWOT Analysis helps identify positive risks you may want to exploit, share, or enhance.

  o Weaknesses lead to threats. A SWOT Analysis helps identify negative risks you may need to avoid, transfer, or mitigate.

Other Tools to Consider

There are other tools pertinent to Business Case development you may wish to consider as well. Here is a quick overview of these tools.

- **Pre-Mortem:** This is a method used to determine what needs to be accomplished in the present based on potential future conditions you try to predict. Look into the future and brainstorm one of two scenarios below.

  - **Scenario 1:** Look into the future. Imagine the organization is highly successful. What actions were taken to achieve this level? Compare the actions you believe were taken to current actions planned. Is there a gap? If so, propose the actions you believe must be taken to achieve future success in your Business Case.

  - **Scenario 2:** Use the same approach in Scenario 1 with one big difference. Imagine your project is complete and failed to meet objectives. Brainstorm reasons why the project may have failed. Determine what actions should have been taken to avoid this failure. Use those actions as potential for your Business Case objectives today!

  - **Sources for a Pre-Mortem:** Key sources of information that can be leveraged include expert input, historical records, Lessons Learned, etc.

- **Influence Diagrams:** This method includes graphical representations of situations showing causal influences, time ordering of events, and other relationships between variables and outcomes. Show influences that can lead to positive results. Show influences that can lead to negative results. Use this information to your advantage in your Business Case.

- **Cause and Effect Diagrams:** Cause and Effect Diagrams show how various causes can result in desired or undesired effects. This method is also referred to as Root Cause and Effect Analysis, Ishikawa Diagraming, and Fishbone Diagramming. Show how your Business Case will address negative root causes that lead to threats, and/or positive root causes that lead to opportunities.

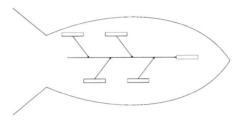

- **Interviews:** Interviews with experts are a great means of gathering information you need in a Business Case. Quotes, supporting statements, and testimonials greatly enhance the credibility of the Business Case.

- **Histograms:** A Histogram is a bar chart that shows events, issues, sales, etc. over a defined time period. A Histogram can provide support for a Business Case as proof of a problem, situation, opportunity, etc. that needs to be addressed. We provide a visual example of a Histogram later in Chapter 9. See Figure 9.2.

- **Pareto Charts:** A Pareto Chart is a vertical bar graph in which values are plotted in decreasing order of relative frequency from left to right. The Pareto Principle contends that 20% of all causes result in 80% of all effects. Pareto Charts are extremely useful for analyzing what problems need attention first because the taller bars on the chart, which represent frequency, clearly illustrate which variables have the greatest cumulative effect on a given system. Figure 7.3 provides an example of a Pareto Chart. This example would be a compelling visual to support a Business Case proposing process changes to reduce shipping times of product to customers.

Figure 7.3 Pareto Chart Example

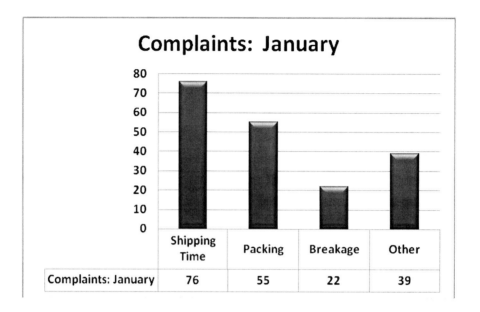

- **Run Charts:** A Run Chart provides a linear view of events or measures over time. Figure 7.4 provides an example of a Run Chart. In this example, CSAT has been steadily decreasing over a six-month period. This Run Chart is a compelling visual if your Business Case proposes actions to increase CSAT.

Figure 7.4 Run Chart Example

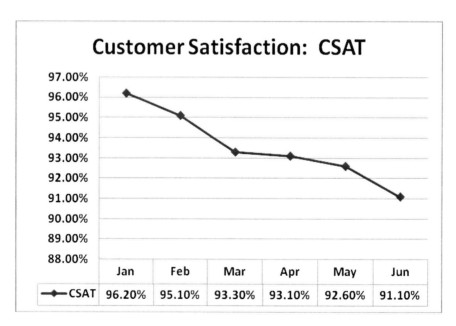

Critical Success Factor(s) (CSF) Analysis

Critical Success Factor(s) (CSF) Analysis drives every organization. A solid Business Case identifies CSF, and analyzes how the organization is meeting them. Many Business Cases present proposals to improve CSF performance.

Every Business Case proposes new products, services, or organizational change. Each Business Case proposal must be compared to the "As Is" state. It is imperative that you show how your proposal, or "To Be" state, is an improvement over the "As Is" state and worth the time and costs to achieve.

Figure 7.5 shows an abbreviated CSF analysis for a Business Case recommending a process improvement solution. The key is to list each CSF, evaluate performance, and compare "As Is" versus "To Be" states. Ensure key stakeholders agree with the assessment, and are willing to support the proposal during the actual Business Case presentation.

Figure 7.5 Sample CSF Analysis Worksheet

ABC Company Change Management Process							
"AS IS"				**"TO BE"**			
Critical Success Factor	**Importance (I)**	**Performance (P)**	**Score (I x P)**	**Critical Success Factor**	**Importance (I)**	**Performance (P)**	**Score (I x P)**
Process Clarity	4	4	16	Process Clarity	4	5	20
Timely Reviews	4	4	16	Timely Reviews	4	5	20
Decision Criteria	5	4	20	Decision Criteria	5	4	20
Status Reporting	3	3	9	Status Reporting	3	4	12
Documentation	3	2	6	Documentation	3	4	12
Change Implementation	5	3	15	Change Implementation	5	4	20
Feedback	4	1	4	Feedback	4	4	16
TOTAL SCORE			86	**TOTAL SCORE**			120

	Importance	Performance			Importance	Performance	
	5: High	5: 100% Effective No Complaints.			5: High	5: 100% Effective No Complaints.	
	4: High to Moderate	4: Some Minor Issues. Effective.			4: High to Moderate	4: Some Minor Issues. Effective.	
Scoring Criteria	3: Moderate	3: Requires Workarounds. Process functional.		**Scoring Criteria**	3: Moderate	3: Requires Workarounds. Process functional.	
	2: Moderate to Low	2: Multiple Major Issues. Process breakdown.			2: Moderate to Low	2: Multiple Major Issues. Process breakdown.	
	1: Low	1: Needs Reengineering. Process 100% ineffective.			1: Low	1: Needs Reengineering. Process 100% ineffective.	

This example documents seven Critical Success Factors for a hypothetical Change Management Process. Each CSF is rated in terms of importance and performance. A score is calculated by multiplying the importance times the performance ratings. Here are some clarifying notes regarding this tool and technique.

- **How Many CSF:** Limit your CSF to the top areas of importance. This example shows seven CSF. Remember that less is more. The more CSF you share, the more potential debate will transpire. Try to refine the list to the top CSF that most stakeholders will acknowledge as important.

- **Importance:** Not all CSF have equal importance in the minds of stakeholders. Some are more important than others. Consult key stakeholders and solicit their input. If four stakeholders provide importance ratings of 4,4,3, and 3, add the numbers and average them. In this example you divide 14/4 = 3.5. Use 3.5 as your score.

- **Performance:** You can expect various performance ratings from a diverse group of stakeholders as well. Some stakeholders may score performance as a five (5). From their standpoint, everything is fine. Others may score performance as a one (1). From their standpoint, the process is broken. The best way to score performance is to use the averaging method discussed above.

  - We used a process improvement project as an example. As such, the performance criterion is process oriented. Change performance criteria to match your desired performance specifics. Just be consistent; score performance for all CSF in a standardized manner. We end this chapter with additional performance rating scales you may wish to use to meet the specific measurement needs of your Business Case. See Figure 7.6.

  - You need to compare the "As Is" to the "To Be" state. Ask "What if" questions. For example, "You scored performance as a three (3). What if we change ABC? How would performance improve?" Record the predicted improvement scores, and average inputs from all stakeholders to determine your "To Be" performance forecasts.

- **Comparing Scores:** The "To Be" score should be higher than the "As Is" score. The larger the range, the better. A CSF Analysis worksheet can show the impact of multiple options. In the example, the "As Is" score is 86. If we implement the Business Case, the "To Be" score will increase to 120 based on stakeholder predictions. If we implement a partial solution, the predicted score will increase to greater than 86, but less than 120.

  o Note 1: There may be times when the "To Be" score is less than the "As Is" score. This data would support disapproval of a proposed project that could lead to creating more problems than it fixes.

  o Note 2: You may have multiple options to offer in your Business Case. If so, score each option separately. Use the overall scores to support the option your Business Case is recommending.

- **Post Implementation Tracking Plan:** The CSF Analysis worksheet can be used to gain approval of your Business Case. For example, we predict an increase in our effectiveness score from 86 to 120 if we approve the project. The CSF Analysis worksheet can also be used to prove you delivered value. Survey or interview stakeholders who provided "As Is" scores, and ask them to score the "To Be" solution after implementation. Did the overall score increase? If so, document the performance score increases and share them as a "win!"

Business Case Tools and Techniques Summary

This concludes our discussion of tools and techniques that help when developing and presenting a Business Case. We leave you with one more figure before we move to our important presentation chapters. Figure 7.6 provides some additional iterations of a performance-scoring chart based on various Business Case objectives.

Figure 7.6 Performance Scoring Options

Customer Service	Time and Resources	Product and Service	CSAT
Performance	Performance	Performance	Performance
5: 100% Effective No Complaints.	5: 100% Effective Meet time and resource plans.	5: Meeting market projections. Sales on upswing.	5: CSAT greater than 90%
4: Few Complaints. Generally Effective.	4: Minor issues. Some time and resource overruns.	4: Sales flattening. May need to upgrade FURPS.	4: CSAT between 85 - 89%
3: High daily volume of complaints. Frustration evident.	3: Satisfactory. Require some workarounds to achieve goals.	3: Sales flat. Need to plan next version or replacement.	3: CSAT between 80 - 84%
2: Major breakdowns. Customers threaten follow up action.	2: Not Effective. Consistent time and resource overruns.	2: Sales declining. Need to retire and expedite replacement.	2: CSAT between 70 - 79%
1: Need to redefine service process. Customers lost.	1: Need to redefine process. Current methods fail	1: Minimal sales. Replacement essential immediately.	1: CSAT less than 70%

Chapter 7 "Food For Thought"

Use the checklist below to determine which Business Case tools and techniques are pertinent to your Business Case.

Tool and Technique	Applicability
Brainstorming	
Nominal Group Technique	
Delphi Technique	
Mind Mapping	
Affinity Charting	
SWOT Analysis	
Pre-Mortem	
Influence Diagrams	
Cause and Effect Diagrams	
Interviews	
CSF Analysis	

My Notes:

Chapter 8: Business Case Presentation Models and Executive Summary

You have probably heard the adage that effective communications requires a combination of adequate preparation *"PLUS"* effective presentation. This is a true statement. There have been many well supported Business Cases that were not approved due to inadequate presentation of what "was" a great idea.

This chapter focuses on the models or templates we recommend you use to present your Business Case. In addition, we end the chapter with an overview of the Business Case Executive Summary.

Before we discuss five proven presentation models, here are some tips to remember:

- **Less is more**: You may be familiar with the "KISS" acronym. When it comes to presenting your Business Case, this acronym stands for "Keep it Short and Sweet." Decision makers are normally higher level executives with limited time. Think "elevator speech." How do I get my proposal on the table in a hurry, gain approval, and begin the real work of making the idea a reality.

- **Be organized:** Follow an organizational pattern that works (that's the premise of this chapter). A common rule of effective presentations states, "Tell them what you will talk about, stay within the subject when you speak, and end with an overview of what you talked about." This method yields results. Getting to the point, and Business Case approval, has a positive correlation. The quicker you get to the point, the greater the chances of approval. On the other hand, the longer you take to get to the point, the lower the chances of approval.

- **Key on What and Why:** Most decision makers want to know "What" you want and "Why" you want it. Do not lead in with the details of "How" you plan to implement your solution. That information is best left in the Appendix of your presentation. Don't be like the salesman who talks too much and loses a sale!

- **PowerPoint:** You may have heard of "Death by PowerPoint." Avoid that syndrome. You can be more effective with a few slides than if you have a lengthy presentation. You need to have support to respond to questions. However, that support belongs in the Appendix. We will include figures that depict how a PowerPoint slide presentation could be developed for a few of the more common presentation methods we will discuss in this chapter.

- **Win as a team:** Try to invite key members of your team to the presentation. Optimally, you should have stakeholders who support the Business Case from the customer standpoint, as well as internal stakeholders with an interest. It is easier for a decision maker to say no to an individual than it is to say no to a team. Consider sharing presentation roles for key testimonials and support. For example, "We shared the value proposition. We invited Elsa Rahim from the ABC organization who will be a primary user of our proposed service to our presentation today. Elsa, could you give us a few words on why this is important to you?"

Common Presentation Templates

There are five common presentation templates we will share that are appropriate for a Business Case presentation. These methods include:

- **5W+H (What, Why, Who, When, Where and How):** This is an appropriate presentation method when there is key information you want to provide in some order of precedence. Format the presentation based on known expectations and information needs of decision makers who will approve or disapprove the Business Case.

- **PNP (Positive, Negative, Positive):** This presentation method is optimal when you want to show how an already positive situation can be further improved upon if a decision maker approves the Business Case. This is also known as the "Good to Great"[3] method as typified in Jim Collin's book *Good to Great*.

---

[3]*Good to Great*, by Jim Collins

- **PIP (Persuade, Inform, Persuade):** This is the "hard sell." You try to sway the decision maker based on a powerful value proposition. You provide supporting information, and follow that with another strong iteration of the value proposition. Have you ever seen an infomercial on television? These marketing attempts are essentially a PIP Business Case to win your business.

- **STP (Situation, Target, Proposal):** This is a very effective template when you have an idea that will improve a negative, or less than optimal, situation. Metrics are critical to the success of this template. Show the decision makers where the organization is on the scorecard versus where it needs to be. For example, "Profit Margin is currently 3%. We require a Profit Margin of 4% to meet our goals." We will provide a PowerPoint tutorial on this template later in the chapter to illustrate this method.

  o **OTP (Opportunity, Target, Proposal):** This is the same as an STP template with one exception. OTP is used when you want to present your proposal as an opportunity to improve upon a product or service that is already performing at a satisfactory level. For example, "We achieved our 4% Profit Margin goal. We have a proposal we strongly believe will increase the Profit Margin to 5%." We group STP/OTP together as a single template for explanation later in this chapter.

- **PSB (Problem, Solution, Benefit):** This is also a very effective template that is best used when there is an acknowledged problem or pain that decision makers understand and recognize the benefit of addressing. For example, "We are all aware that sales have suffered in the past two months. We have a proposed solution that will elevate sales levels and greatly improve overall profitability." We also provide a PowerPoint tutorial on this method later in the chapter as well.

5W+H: What, Why, Who, When, and How

The 5W+H presentation method works well when you have key information you want to provide in some priority order based on audience informational needs. The 5W+H stands for "What, Why, Who, When, Where, and How."

The 5W+H method is most effective when you have an understanding of who the audience consists of, and understand their expectations. We discuss a method of how people think and behave later in Chapter 9 called Emergenetics. This overview should help you determine the optimal mix of what, why, who, when, where, and how information to address in your Business Case. Always begin with "What" and "Why" information if you have no idea who the audience consists of. This is a low risk approach that normally works.

- **Applicability:** Your Business Case has a lot of key points. Your goal is to pick the most important points to present to decision makers. Tailor your choices to the decision maker's needs. If possible, do some research ahead of time to determine what information is most important to the key stakeholders you are presenting to. Learn as much as you can to improve chances of success.

- **Method:** Introduce your idea. Substantiate your idea with key 5W+H points the decision makers are interested in. Close out the presentation. See Figure 8.1 for an abbreviated 5W+H presentation example.

- **Tips:** Follow the five-step approach provided in Figure 8.1. We will elaborate more on this approach in Chapter 9.

  o Remember to strive for brevity. Provide enough information to share key points. Don't oversell.

  o Have supporting information available. If you use information you cannot substantiate, you risk losing credibility.

  o Be ready for questions. How you respond can make the difference between success and failure. We will share more on responding to questions effectively in Chapter 9 as well.

Figure 8.1 5W+H Presentation Example

Business Case Objective	Add a New Feature to an Existing Software Application to Improve Reliability	
Step 1: Opening	**Share Objective**	• State "What" you are proposing. • In this example, you are proposing a new feature. Provide a high-level overview of the feature. Avoid providing too much information.
Step 2: Value Proposition	**Share a High-level Value Proposition:** For example, CSAT is down. Customer complaints are on the rise. Our last VOC survey revealed this need.	• Summarize into short overview of total value proposition. Tell them what you will share. • In this example, there may be an opportunity to reduce complaints and improve CSAT. • Let decisions makers know you have supporting data. • Prepare for questions.
Step 3: Share 5W+H Criteria	1. **What:** Customers are asking for new functionality to be added to our application. 2. **Who:** We have been approached by partners from the XYZ Corporation and ABC group. 3. **When:** Our goal is to add the additional functionality and launch in Q3.	• In this example, we chose key what, who, and when considerations. We could have added where, or how considerations had they been more pertinent. • Add some support for each factor. Maintain the majority of support in the Appendix.
Step 4: Summarize	**Review Key Points:** Reiterate the Key Value Proposition.	• Recap the presentation. "Tell them what you told them."
Step 5: Close	**Closure**	• Ask for approval or propose next steps.

PNP: Positive, Negative, Positive

The PNP presentation method works best when you are performing well, but believe you have an opportunity to improve. The PNP acronym stands for "Positive, Negative, Positive." Open the presentation with a positive overview of performance. Follow with an improvement idea. Close with an overview of potential levels of success you believe you can achieve.

- **Applicability:** This Business Case style is applicable to many scenarios.

  o PNP is widely used to sell employees and customers on change. We are doing well today—but we can do better tomorrow. Here's the issue!

  o PNP can be used to overcome potential resistance from stakeholders who contributed to the current process, service, methods, etc. It is easier to gain support when you want to go from good to great than to depict the current "As Is" state as negative.

  o PNP is a winner when you want to motivate good employees to improve performance. You begin by thanking them for their current level of effort and results. You then challenge them to perform at a higher level, and share your belief that they can achieve the higher goal.

- **Method:** Introduce your proposal. Begin with an overview of the positive state. Share the improvement proposal and show how the organization can do even better. See Figure 8.2 for an abbreviated PNP presentation example.

- **Tips:** PNP does not work in every case. It is most appropriate for good to great proposals.

  o Don't try to put a positive slant on a totally negative situation. People will see through this strategy, and you may be perceived as disingenuous.

  o Don't oversell the initial positive overview, or set false expectations for the level of greatness you can achieve. Remember the SMARTWAY formula we shared earlier. Objectives should be attainable and yield the promised results.

Figure 8.2 PNP Presentation Example

Business Case Objective	Improve Work Life Integration by Adding an Employee Benefits Feature	
Step 1: Opening	**Share Objective**	• State "What" you are proposing. • Share the fact the current program is good but can be elevated. Key word— "Improve."
Step 2: Value Proposition	**Share a High-level Value Proposition:** For example, we have great benefits in our company. However, we can improve the package for our families. If we do, Work Life Integration will improve even more!	• Summarize into short overview of total value proposition. Tell them what you will share. • In this example, there may be an opportunity to improve Work Life Integration by adding a new benefit that supports the family. • Prepare for questions.
Step 3: Share PNP Criteria	1. **Where We Are:** Share the positive nature of the current program. 2. **Where We Want to Go:** Share how adding the new benefit will take the organization from good to great. 3. **Solidify the Proposal:** End on a positive note. Show how the proposal is attainable, relevant, and will yield results.	• Use the mountain analogy. Our current program gets us half-way up the mountain. Our new proposal will take us to the top. The top is "a better place to be." • Add some support for each factor. Maintain the majority of support in the Appendix.
Step 4: Summarize	**Review Key Points:** Reiterate the PNP Value Proposition.	• Recap the presentation. "Tell them what you told them."
Step 5: Close	**Closure**	• Ask for approval, or propose next steps.

PIP: Persuade, Inform, Persuade

The PIP presentation method works well when you believe you have a compelling value proposition that needs to be fulfilled without delay. The acronym stands for "Persuade, Inform, and Persuade." This method expresses a level of urgency to achieve a critically important solution as quickly as possible.

- **Applicability:** This Business Case style is applicable to scenarios when you believe there is a critical value proposition that needs to be achieved now. It is appropriate when you want to create urgency around the criticality of your proposed solution.

- **Method:** Introduce your proposal. Begin with a key value proposition that is critical to achieve. Share basic information as required to substantiate your value proposition and the need for implementation of the proposed solution. End with a "bang!" Reiterate the value proposition and express a level of urgency to achieve the objective. See Figure 8.3 for an abbreviated PIP presentation example.

- **Tips:** PIP does not work for every Business Case. It is most appropriate for proposals with a critical value proposition that must be accomplished at the earliest possible time. This is not a good approach for more routine proposals.

  - Do your homework. Make sure your argument is compelling enough to convince the decision maker that the proposal truly is critical and must be achieved quickly.

  - Validate the criticality of achieving the proposal's value proposition with others. A PIP proposal generally needs support. There is safety in numbers. There is a high-level of danger in advocating a position when others do not share your passion, urgency, and enthusiasm.

  - Don't try to create a level of urgency if there is no real reason to do so. Try to gain support from key stakeholders who are willing to substantiate the need to achieve a solution quickly.

Figure 8.3 PIP Presentation Example

Business Case Objective	Initiate an Immediate Marketing Campaign to Regain Lost Market Share	
Step 1: Opening	Share Objective	• State "What" you are proposing. • Show a sense of urgency to achieve the objective.
Step 2: Value Proposition	**Share a Compelling Value Proposition:** For example, Market share has decreased by over 10% in the last quarter. This is due to a new competitor's product. We need to launch an immediate marketing campaign to show how our product competes.	• Provide rationale behind your urgency. • Provide a compelling "Why" statement, and the impact of not acting now. • Solicit support from other stakeholders. • Prepare for questions.
Step 3: Share PIP Criteria	1. **Persuade:** Elaborate on the objective and reason why implementation is critical. 2. **Inform:** Provide supporting data to substantiate the proposal. 3. **Persuade:** Share benefits to the organization of acting swiftly.	• PIP can be summarized as "We have a critical issue, here's the facts, now let's fix it fast!" • Add some support for each factor. Maintain the majority of support in the Appendix.
Step 4: Summarize	**Review Key Points:** Recommend approval of the proposal.	• Recap the presentation. "Tell them what you told them." • Reiterate the request for approval. • Consider using a key stakeholder with influence to present the summary.
Step 5: Close	Closure	• Ask for approval, or propose next steps.

STP or OTP: Situation/Opportunity, Target, Proposal

STP or OTP is the acronym for the "Situation, Target, Proposal" (STP) or "Opportunity, Target, Proposal" (OTP) presentation template. These methods are highly effective when you have quantitative data or metrics to substantiate a proposal.

- **Applicability:** STP works best when the numbers are lower than satisfactory. For example, "Market share is currently 33%. We set a target of 40% by the end of this year." OTP works best when your numbers are meeting expectations. However, there is an opportunity to perform at an even higher level. For example, "We met our goal of $80,000 in sales for the last quarter. We have an opportunity to increase sales beyond that current goal next quarter."

- **Method:** Quantify your situation or opportunity with a key metric that decision makers agree is important. Compare the "As Is" to the "To Be", or optimal state. That metric is represented as the target you believe your proposal will achieve. Finalize the Business Case presentation with your proposal, and share the benefits you believe achieving the target will yield.

- **Tips:** STP or OTP are highly effective when you have quantifiable data on which to base your Business Case. Some tips to keep in mind are as follows.

  - Ensure data presented to express a situation, opportunity or target are supportable. Do not pull the numbers "out of the hat" so to speak.

  - Solicit input and support of key stakeholders who are willing to validate the importance and benefits of reaching the proposed target.

  - Perform a Cost Benefit Analysis whenever applicable. For example, you may propose an automation project that increases reliability from 98.5% to 99.5%. Make sure that the benefits you will gain justify the cost of achieving the new target.

Figure 8.4 shows a sample STP or OTP presentation. Figure 8.5 shows how a PowerPoint slide show could be developed to support your Business Case.

Figure 8.4 STP or OTP Presentation Example

Business Case Objective	Improve Customer Satisfaction (CSAT) by Implementing a Voice of the Customer (VOC) Program	
Step 1: Opening	**Share Objective**	• State "What" you propose. • If the current situation is not meeting expectations use STP. • If you are meeting expectations and, believe you can exceed them, use OTP.
Step 2: Overview and Value Proposition	**Provide an overview:** For example: We believe we have an opportunity to increase CSAT by 10% by implementing a new VOC program.	• Provide an overview of your STP or OTP proposal. • Share a brief overview of a key value proposition up-front. • Prepare for questions.
Step 3: Share STP/OTP Criteria	1. **Situation or Opportunity:** Where is the organization today? For example, CSAT is 85%. 2. **Target:** Where does the organization need to be? For example 95%. 3. **Proposal:** What is your proposal to improve CSAT? Why does it matter?	• Cover each category in order. This method can be summarized by the statement, "Here's where we are, here's where we need to be, and here's how we'll get there." • Share "Why" achieving the target is important. • Add some support for each factor. Maintain the majority of support in the Appendix.
Step 4: Summarize	**Review Key Points:** Recommend approval of the proposal. Share a key benefit. Share other options considered.	• Recap the presentation. "Tell them what you told them." • Request approval. • Share other options considered. • Reiterate a key benefit of reaching the target. • Consider using a key stakeholder with influence to help present the summary.
Step 5: Close	**Closure**	• Reiterate request for approval, or propose next steps.

STP or OTP Presentation Example in PowerPoint

Figure 8.5 is a sample STP or OTP PowerPoint presentation example you can adapt to your Business Case. The first two slides are critically important. Introduce your objective as quickly as possible on Slide 1 and get to the point. Slide 2 serves as an overview slide, and as an insurance policy.

There are times when the thirty minutes you thought you had for your Business Case presentation turns into five minutes. If you need to adjust your presentation into a quick elevator speech, Slide 2 tells the whole story at a high-level.

It is recommended you include a quick value proposition during your overview on Slide 2. If your value proposition is compelling, your presentation may end quickly with approval on the spot. Sometimes less is more. This can work to your advantage.

Note that the majority of your Business Case will be described in the Appendix slides. This concept will also hold true for the PSB presentation we feature in the next section. Analyze your audience, determine what they need to hear, and provide that information. The best Business Case presentation is one that is developed with the audience's informational needs in mind.

As a final reminder, remember that the STP presentation format is best when you want to address an area for potential improvement. It is normally used when you are not meeting expectations. OTP is used when you are meeting expectations. This format is effective to show how you can "move the dial" even higher.

Figure 8.5 STP or OTP PowerPoint Example

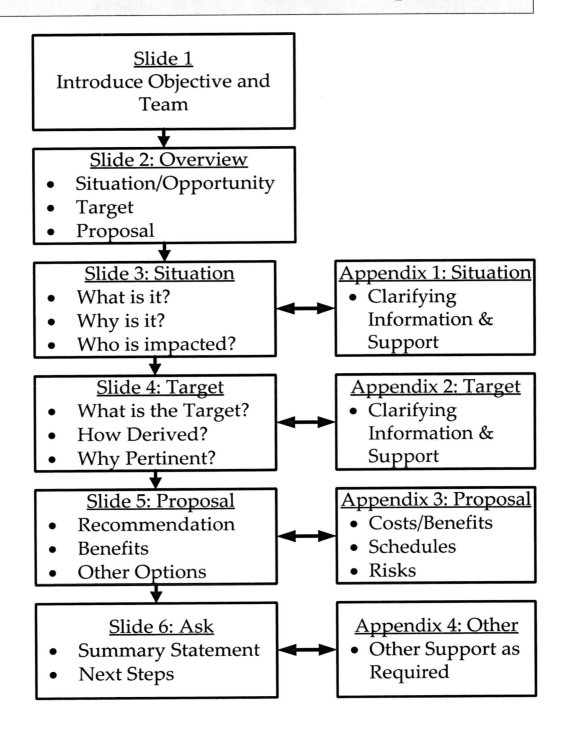

PSB: Problem, Solution, Benefits

The last presentation method we will discuss is PSB. PSB is an acronym that stands for "Problem, Solution, and Benefits" (PSB).

- **Applicability:** PSB is the method most appropriate when there is an acknowledged problem that needs to be solved. The emphasis of this presentation method is on choosing the right solution with the greatest benefits.

- **Method:** Share your objective and any support needed to substantiate your assessment of the problem.

  o The overview of the problem should not take long. In most cases, this segment is a reminder that there is a problem, and validation that the problem is still important enough to address.

  o Share your solution and the benefits associated with your recommendation. Be prepared to show how doing nothing by choosing "As Is" compares to the "To Be" benefits expected to be gained through your solution.

- **Tips:**

  o Ensure decision makers agree with your problem assessment. Solicit problem validation from key stakeholders as necessary. You may want to "Apply the Grease" before your presentation. Gain validation the problem is a priority to solve prior to presenting your Business Case. Priorities do sometimes change. Don't be caught by surprise.

  o Provide at least three options to include the "As Is" state. Support your solution as the optimal choice. Remember that the "status quo" is sometimes the right choice.

Figure 8.6 shows a sample PSB presentation. Figure 8.7 shows how a PowerPoint presentation could be developed to support your Business Case.

Figure 8.6 PSB Presentation Example

Business Case Objective	Reduce Time Required to Quality Control (QC) Products Prior to Shipment	
Step 1: Opening	**Share Objective**	• State your objective and introduce the team. • Transition quickly to the PSB overview.
Step 2: Overview	**Provide an overview:** For example: Customers are complaining about the time required to ship products. We have a proposal to improve ship times by reducing QC time.	• Provide a problem statement that will solicit agreement. • Make the promise of a solution—no detail required. • Share the key reason or benefit to undertake the objective.
Step 3: Share PSB Criteria	1. **Problem:** Current QC process time is excessive. Shipping is delayed. 2. **Solution:** Automate manual tracking and recording systems 3. **Benefits:** Improve time to market. Satisfy customer requirements.	• Address each category in order. This method can be summarized by the statement, "Here's the problem, here's the solution, and here's why it's important." • Add some support for each factor. Maintain the majority of support in the Appendix.
Step 4: Summarize	**Review Key Points:** Recommend approval of the proposal. Share a key benefit. Share other options considered.	• Recap the presentation. "Tell them what you told them." • Reiterate the request for approval. • Reiterate the benefits of reaching the target. • Consider using a key stakeholder with influence to present the summary.
Step 5: Close	**Closure**	• Ask for approval, or propose next steps.

Figure 8.7 PSB PowerPoint Example

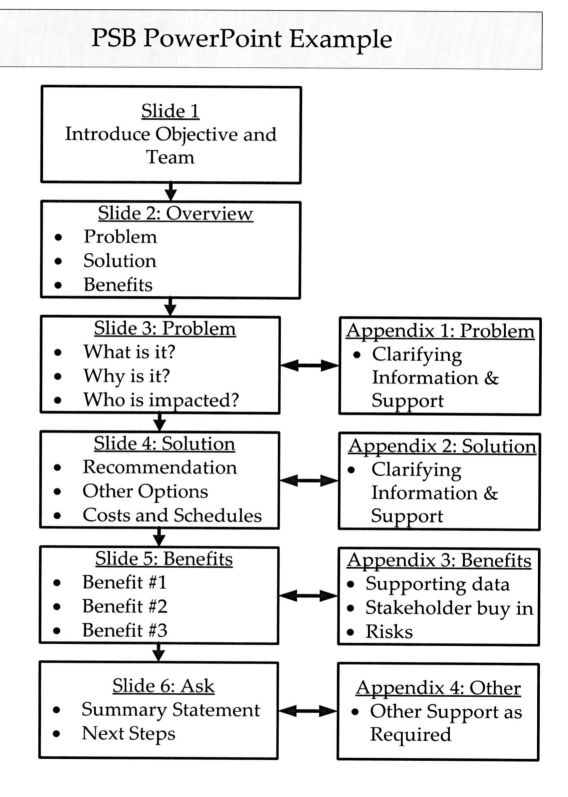

Figure 8.7 is a sample PSB PowerPoint presentation you can adapt to your Business Case. Once again the first two slides are critical. You need to share an objective to solve a problem that all decision makers agree needs to be solved. Your overview slide puts your entire proposal in front of decision makers quickly. This is essential as you may have limited time to get to the point of your Business Case.

There are a number of common questions you can anticipate. They include, "What are our other options? How much will this cost? What are the returns compared to the costs? When can we make this happen?" These considerations are addressed in the template.

The Business Case Executive Summary

A formal Executive Summary should be part of every Business Case. This is normally the first description of your Business Case that decision makers and stakeholders read.

The Executive Summary is one of the last parts of the Business Case you complete. It is best to wait until you have all key pieces of information documented, and your Business Case relatively complete, to ensure you are able to choose the most pertinent information regarding your proposal.

An overview of a sample Business Case Executive Summary is provided in Figure 8.8. Note that the Executive Summary format differs from the Business Case format. The number one question decision makers want to know up-front is "What is your proposal?" Respond to that question first, and then finalize the rest of the summary to support the proposal. A few tips before we share the example:

- **Be brief**: Your Executive Summary should normally not exceed a single page.

- **Consider multiple iterations**: You may want to develop multiple iterations of the Executive Summary for various audiences. What is important to internal stakeholders may differ from what external stakeholders believe is important.

- **Edit your work**: Enlist support from trusted associates to check the Executive Summary for readability, content, impact, and accuracy.

- **Pre-coordinate:** Use your Executive Summary to pre-coordinate or "Apply the Grease" as we previously discussed prior to your formal Business Case presentation. The Executive Summary is a quick way to gain initial support for a proposal.

Figure 8.8 Sample Business Case Executive Summary

Component Breakout	Summary
Proposal: What is my objective and goal?	- Share bottom-line solution and objective. - Example: Invest $20,000 to develop a Customer Service Center for key partners. This will improve overall CPE.
Costs and Benefits: Provide high-level costs and benefits.	- Cost and investment requirements. When are investment funds required? - Benefits schedule. When will benefits be realized? - Financial metrics: ROI, IRR, NPV, etc.
Stakeholder Impact: Who will this proposal impact?	- Who is impacted? - Who is supportive? - Are there resistance/adoption issues?
Schedule: When do you plan to implement the proposal?	- High-level schedule. - Phased approach works well—see the WBS example provided in Chapter 6.
Risks: Define high-level risks and planned responses.	- Top 3 risks and planned responses. - Choose risks based on known stakeholder tolerances.
Ask: What do you need?	- What decision is required from stakeholders?

Business Case Presentation Models Summary

This concludes our chapter on Business Case models or templates. We provided basic models and shared the applicability of each. These models can be used and adapted to meet your specific Business Case needs. We highly recommend you use these models. They provide an organized approach that decision makers will recognize and appreciate. They are designed to improve chances of a successful Business Case presentation, and achievement of your goals.

We also provided an overview and sample of a Business Case Executive Summary. Complete this segment of the Business Case at the end of your development cycle when you have all the information you need. Choose the most pertinent information to sell your Business Case's merits.

We now shift our attention to techniques you can apply during the actual presentation itself. You have a solid Business Case. You developed a great presentation. It's now time to deliver the presentation effectively. Let's move forward to Chapter 9!

Chapter 8 "Food For Thought"

Part I:

Use the checklist below to determine the presentation technique that is most pertinent to your Business Case. Also, use this template for notes and preparation.

Presentation Step and Criteria	Notes
Opening: What is my objective?	
Overview: What is my #1 Value Proposition?	
Body: Which presentation template best matches my proposal? STP, PSB, etc.?	
Summary: What is the most important point I want the audience to remember?	
Close: What feedback do I expect?	

Part II:

Use the template below to determine if you have enough information to develop your Business Case Executive Summary.

Component Breakout	Summary
Proposal: What is my objective and goal?	
Costs and Benefits: Provide high-level costs and benefits.	
Stakeholder Impact: Who will this proposal impact?	
Schedule: When do you plan to implement the proposal?	
Risks: Define high-level risks and planned responses.	
Ask: What do you need?	

My Notes:

Chapter 9: Effective Business Case Presentation Techniques

The mechanics of developing a Business Case and formatting the presentation are critical to success. Equally critical is how you present. This chapter will explore, in detail, a five-step presentation approach that will not fail you. Figure 9.1 outlines the five-steps. These steps may seem easy at first sight. However, there's far more than meets the eyes. Let's explore both the art and science of effective presenting.

Figure 9.1 Effective Presenting—a 5-Step Approach

Effective Presenting—a 5-Step Approach	
Step 1: Attention	←→ Share a compelling "What"
Step 2: Motivation & Overview	←→ Tell the audience "Why". Give them the "WII-FM"
Step 3: Body	←→ Use a three-step approach. "Rule of 3"
Step 4: Remotivation	←→ Reinforce the "Why"
Step 5: Conclusion & Next Steps	←→ Share the "Ask"

Step 1: Capturing the Audience's Attention

Have you ever listened to a presentation that seemingly had no direction or purpose? If you've been in business for any length of time at all, this is a rhetorical question. The answer is of course, yes. We all have experienced this type of presentation.

You have a small window of opportunity when you begin your Business Case presentation to either capture the attention of the stakeholders in attendance, or lull them into a state of disinterest, boredom, and a search for an exit strategy. First impressions are lasting. You need to make your first impression hit home.

There are a number of keys to success we can share. There are "best" and "worst" practices. Let's discuss positive attention-step strategies that will help you win the day.

- **Definitive Statement:** Provide a compelling statement of fact that you know is of interest to the audience. Catch their attention. For example, open your presentation with "The number of customer complaints for July increased by 40%. This is an alarming trend we need to address." This opening is far more compelling than, "Good morning, my name is Dale Nelson and I want to talk about customer complaints."

- **Rhetorical Question:** Pose a question to the group with an obvious answer. The answer to the question, however, should resonate with the audience. For example, "How many of us in this room would prefer to talk with a frustrated customer instead of a satisfied one?" Always pause for a moment after using a rhetorical question to allow time for the audience to think and digest the meaning. Your follow up statement would be, "No one of course. Today I am here to talk about a dramatic increase in the number of customer complaints we received in July and hopefully gain approval for a solid plan our team developed to reduce them." Use some caution when using a rhetorical question. Try to avoid talking down to the audience, or insulting their intelligence. Share your idea with a friend before you try it. Safety first!

- **Visual:** A visual is an incredibly powerful attention step when your choice has credibility and meaning. For example, a customer complaint scenario is illustrated below. You may want to use the definitive statement or the rhetorical question in conjunction with a visual. Make sure, however, that the data you share in the visual is accurate. Figure 9.2 shows how a graph of complaints can be quite compelling. This example is referred to as a Histogram.

Figure 9.2 Visual Example (Histogram)

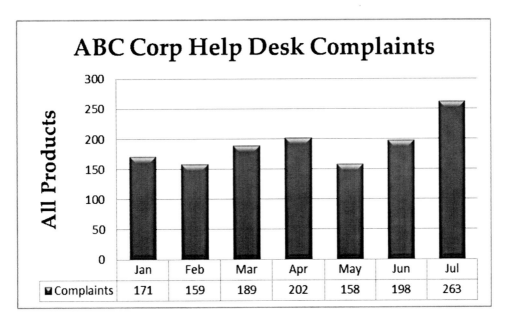

- **Share the Problem, Situation, or Opportunity Up-Front:** The STP, OTP, and PSB models discussed in the previous chapter have built in attention statements. Use these models to your advantage:

  o **Problem:** For example, "Customer complaints have increased dramatically over the past month. We have a solution to this problem that will yield results and benefits to share with you today."

  o **Situation:** For example, "Customer complaints increased 40% during July to 263. This is well above our target of 150 or below. As a matter of fact, we have not achieved our goal once in the past six months."

- o **Opportunity:** For example, "We have an opportunity to reduce complaints below their current levels, and perhaps even below our goal of 150 or less per month. Our team would like to share a proposal that we believe will allow us to be successful."

The attention step is important. It is your opportunity to get the audience to focus on you rather than the many other issues that are likely on their minds. Be creative, be confident, but don't go overboard. If you can capture their attention for a moment, the motivational step we discuss next allows you to keep it.

Step 2: Motivating the Audience and Providing an Overview

Have you ever listened to WII-FM? Most people have. However, this is not an FM radio station as we shared earlier. It's a voice inside everyone that asks, "What's in it for me?"

We shared the four perspectives of the Balanced Scorecard model in Chapter 3. Your Business Case likely impacts multiple perspectives, and presents various value propositions. Remember this key point. All value propositions are not equal in the minds of decision makers. One decision maker may value customer perspective enhancements highest. Others may value financial perspective value propositions highest. You have three critical jobs in Step 2. First, analyze your audience. Second, determine which "Why" factor will have the greatest potential to influence them. Third, provide a brief overview of what you will discuss in your presentation to provide direction, share objectives and set audience expectations.

The Emergenetics ® Model

Geil Browning, PhD, developed the Emergenetics Model. Geil describes Emergenetics as, "a brain-based approach to personality profiling that gives you the keys to discover not only your own natural strengths and talents, but also those of others." Application of Emergenetics allows you to "make presentations that appeal to everyone, sell to all kinds of customers, and motivate all kinds of employees."[4] I highly encourage you to go to the Emergenetics website and take a profile. You will learn a lot about what makes you the unique person you are![5] There is a nominal cost. But the results are worth the investment.

---

[4] *Emergenetics*, Geil Browning, PhD
[5] www.emergenetics.com

Your motivation and overview step is an opportunity to keep the attention of your audience and motivate them to listen. This step should take no more than one minute. Emergenetics teaches us about effective ways to communicate and win during this important one-minute segment. Figure 9.3 shares four thinking attributes that drive people's thought processes.

Figure 9.3 Emergenetics Four Thinking Attributes

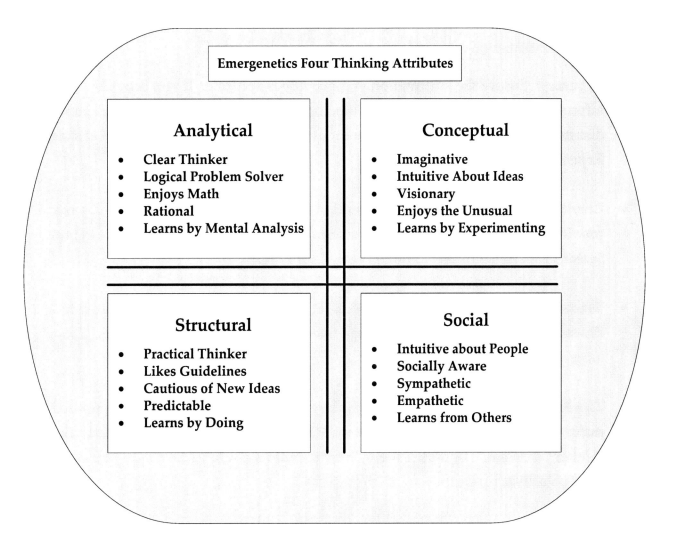

Grabbing the Attention of the Analytical Thinker

According to Emergenetics, approximately 68% of all of the hundreds of thousands of people who completed Emergenetics profiles have a preference for analytical thinking (See Figure 9.4 at the end of this section for a breakout of combinations of thinking attribute combinations). This percentage increases as you move up higher on the corporate organizational chart. Analytical thinkers are logical, objective, rational, and love to get to the point quickly. Here are some things to consider throughout your presentation to capture the attention, motivate, and win over the analytical mind.

- **Accuracy:** Ensure the information you provide is accurate. If you provide information that cannot be substantiated or proven, your presentation will become a disaster. Have back up support data for every piece of key information you share! Expect challenges.

- **Brevity:** You need to finish your attention and motivation steps quickly. Do not provide more information than necessary. Remember "KISS": Keep it Short and Sweet. This rule definitely applies here. Less is more.

- **Executive Summary:** Follow the PSB, STP, or alternative templates we provided. Provide the analytical thinker with the Executive Summary ahead of time. If they have questions, they will ask.

- **The Facts—Just the Facts:** Provide the key pieces of information that are needed to make the decision. "This is what we want to do. This is why." Tell the analytical thinker "the time." Don't tell them "how to build a clock." Make sure you explain your objectives up-front.

- **Do the Math:** The analytical thinker will definitely review your financial metrics to determine cost versus benefits. Be prepared for some questions in this area. Have support data available.

- **Present Logical, Data-Based Conclusions:** PSB and STP are superb templates to win over the analytical thinker. They present your Business Case in a logical manner that makes sense.

- **Time to Digest:** Give the analytical thinker time to understand and digest information. Providing your PowerPoint presentation ahead of time is also a best practice.

- **Allow Time for Questions:** Analytical thinkers will have questions. Some may be tough. Anticipate them. We provide some tips on answering questions later in this chapter.

The analytical thinker is your most likely audience. Prepare accordingly. Remember to apply the ABC rule—"Be Accurate, Brief, and Concise."

Grabbing the Attention of the Structural Thinker

According to Emergenetics, approximately 55% of all who have completed Emergenetics profiles have a preference for structural thinking (See Figure 9.4). Structural thinkers are practical, detail oriented, methodical, and thorough. They follow guidelines, rules, policies, and are able to create order from the chaos. Here are some tips to consider throughout your presentation to capture the attention, motivate, and win over the structural mind.

- **Facts and Details:** Ensure you have all the facts and details to support your proposal available for review. These items are best placed in the presentation Appendix. The Structural Thinker will likely review them. Expect questions.

- **Agenda and Outline:** Do not forget the agenda or outline for your presentation. In addition, ALWAYS provide an overview of your presentation and follow it faithfully. The Structural thinker will hold you to the promised plan.

- **No Surprises:** Consider sharing your game plan and expectations with the structural thinker ahead of time. Do not change things during the presentation on your own unless absolutely necessary. Structural thinkers dislike surprises.

- **On-Track and On-Time:** Follow your presentation as you built it. If you have 30 minutes to present, set a goal to finish on time. Structural thinkers will start looking at their watches if you begin to run over.

- **Show the Fit:** If possible, show how your proposal complements current organizational processes, guidelines, procedures, values, etc.

- **Questions:** Allow time in your presentation for questions and answers.

The structural thinker will likely be part of your audience. As a matter of fact, about 36% of all people have preferences in both the analytical and structural thinking areas! Following the direction we have provided for developing and presenting your Business Case will greatly increase your chances of success.

Grabbing the Attention of the Conceptual Thinker

According to Emergenetics, approximately 51% of Emergenetics profiles show a preference for conceptual thinking (See Figure 9.4). Conceptual thinkers are visionaries, consider the big picture, embrace new ideas, consider all impacts, and look into the future. Here are some things to consider throughout your presentation to capture the attention, motivate, and win over the conceptual thinker.

- **Brainstorm:** Conceptual thinkers love to take an idea, and Brainstorm to find all the possibilities. Allow some time in your presentation for discussion and questions.

- **Big Picture:** You need to show how your proposal fits into the overall organizational vision up-front. Show them the "fit." Do not jump into the details unless asked. The conceptual thinker may mentally check out of the room.

- **Plan for Tangents:** The conceptual thinker may inadvertently divert your presentation. You may want to use the "Parking Lot" concept to keep your presentation on-track. For example, "That is a great thought. Let me write that down and get back with you. I think we definitely need to consider this in our final solution."

- **Be Thorough:** Spend time on the advantages and disadvantages of your proposal. Pay special attention to risks and potential risk responses. The conceptual thinker will look at the big picture, and question you if any key considerations are missed.

- **Flexible, Scalable, and Future Oriented:** One of the conceptual thinker's greatest gifts is to analyze a solution for its impact today and tomorrow. Ensure you avoid presenting a solution that is "locked in stone." Provide a foundational proposal, and show options for modifying, scaling, and improving in the future. Be open to new ideas.

- **Creativity and Inventiveness:** The conceptual thinker is going to provide some great ideas and food for thought to take your proposal from good, to great and greater. Listen closely, and take advantage of this creativity and inventiveness. The ideas are often spot on!

The conceptual thinker can help you take your initial proposal to the next level. Understand the conceptual thinker's viewpoint, and be prepared to address their considerations.

Don't lose focus of what a Business Case represents. It is a high-level proposal that is presented in hopes of turning a great idea into a project. Your solution is not, and should not, be finalized and inflexible at the Business Case stage. The goal is approval to initiate and plan a project that will move your organization or company forward in a way that positively impacts any and all four of the Balanced Scorecard perspectives previously discussed.

Grabbing the Attention of the Social Thinker

According to Emergenetics, approximately 61% of completed Emergenetics profiles have a preference for social thinking (See Figure 9.4). Social thinkers are empathetic and intuitive about people. They are able to communicate difficult messages, and think about the cause and effect of actions on people. Here are some things to consider throughout your presentation to capture the attention, motivate, and win over the social thinker.

- **Gain Input:** It is optimal to gain input for your Business Case from stakeholders who are social thinkers. They will appreciate the courtesy you show, and likely be advocates of your proposal during the presentation.

- **Introductions:** Introduce the members of your team, if applicable, at some point during the presentation. The optimal time to do so is after your attention and motivation steps.

- **Non-Verbal Communications:** Watch your body language, facial expressions, etc. Smile and show passion. You may lose the social thinker if you become frustrated, sarcastic, or disingenuous. Leave any frustration at the door.

- **The People Factor:** Adoption risks for changes your proposal will institute are a key consideration moving forward. The social thinker can help you tremendously in understanding the people impact of your proposal and how to effectively address those key considerations.

Enlisting the support of the social thinker is imperative. They are passionate about the impact of ideas on customers and employees--two critical Balanced Scorecard perspectives you want to enhance.

Figure 9.4 Emergenetics Thinking Attribute Combinations and Percentages

Emergenetics Thinking Attribute Percentages (Rounded)				
Thinking Attribute Combination	Analytical (A)	Structural (T)	Conceptual (C)	Social (S)
A, T, C, S	1%	1%	1%	1%
A, T	17%	17%		
S, C			12%	12%
A, C	12%		12%	
T, S		11%		11%
A, S	6%			6%
T, C		2%	2%	
A, T, S	13%	13%		13%
A, C, S	13%		13%	13%
T, C, S		4%	4%	4%
A, T, C	5%	5%	5%	
A	1%			
T		2%		
C			2%	
S				1%
TOTAL	**68%**	**55%**	**51%**	**61%**

Note 1: The percentages in this table do not add up to 100%. This is due to rounding.

Note 2: Percentages are based on over 250,000 Emergenetics profiles processed and analyzed through 2006.[6]

---

[6] *Emergenetics*, Browning, Copyright 2006

Step 1 and 2 Summary

The motivation and overview step partners with your attention step to set the stage for a positive and successful presentation. Use these steps to your advantage to catch the attention and motivate the audience to listen to what you are about to share. Here is a summary of tips to this point.

- **Time:** Do not spend more than one minute on your attention, motivation, and overview steps. The audience can read your slides faster than you can speak. They will "get it" through a combination of your words, and the text on the slides you provide. You may get some questions at this point. Ensure the audience you will cover the questions in a few minutes and ask for their patience. Here's a great approach, "The short answer to your question is yes. I will cover that in just a few minutes in greater detail on the next slide if that's OK." In most cases, you'll get an "OK."

- **The Short Story:** A key to success is to ensure the audience has a high-level overview of what you will talk about, and the purpose of your presentation. In some cases, you may be asked to complete your presentation during the overview slide. That can be positive. It is not improbable that the key decision maker will state, "I think we all concur with your approach and proposal. I've read through the Business Case and I'm ready to approve the next steps unless anyone has any issues." You may get a few questions—but that's fine. Smile, say thank you, and move forward.

- **What and Why:** The key points you need to share are the "What" and "Why" of your Business Case. "This is what we propose and why." Your overview allows you the opportunity to share a few words about how the presentation will unfold, provide your objectives on a single PowerPoint slide, and motivate the audience at the same time. We discuss the details of the actual presentation in Step 3 of the five-step presentation process.

- **The Refusal:** You may possibly encounter a negative response to your proposal during the Business Case presentation. We will share some tips on how to handle a non-supportive or even hostile audience later in this chapter. If the presentation does turn negative, or your feedback is a "no" answer, remember these tips.

  o Don't become angry or emotional. Maintain your professionalism, and acknowledge the dissenter's opinions.

  o Ask if there is anything you can do to overcome the objections, and get the idea back on the table. Share your courage and conviction, and enlist the support of other stakeholders who share your support of the proposal to provide their thoughts.

- **Be Aware of Different Thinking Styles:** There are different thinking styles you will encounter. You need to satisfy them all in the first minutes of your presentation. As a quick review:

  o **Analytical:** Be sure your information is accurate. Have data to support your proposal. Show the Return on Investment (ROI) of your proposal up-front. Use bullet statements—don't jump into the details immediately. Share objectives.

  o **Structural:** Be organized. Provide an agenda, overview, and follow the promised plan in your presentation as much as possible. Stress the practicality of your solution up-front. Have details available if needed.

  o **Conceptual:** Show how your proposal fits into the big picture. Let the audience know up-front that your proposal is flexible, scalable, and will endure the test of time.

  o **Social:** Introduce your team. Smile, say hello, and break the ice. Let the audience know up-front that the impact on people was considered and will be addressed. Show team solidarity. Be yourself and talk with the audience—not at them.

Step 3: Present the Body of Your Presentation

Steps one (1) and two (2) set you up for success in Step three (3). This is where you present the majority of your proposal. Here are some tips to be successful as you present.

- **Follow your outline:** Try not to deviate from the overview you provided. Stay the course. If you change direction at this point, some structural thinkers in the audience may become frustrated. If you do need to add something, try to respond and get back on-track as quickly as possible.

- **Leverage best practices in presenting:** Use your voice, gestures, and body language to your advantage. We provide more detailed information later in this chapter. In particular, watch your voice and body language. Social thinkers are listening, watching, and evaluating. Keep them on your side. Maintain their support.

- **Be brief:** Provide all Business Case information in an abbreviated form. Use bullets in your slides, and talk to the bullets. Do not read your slides. The majority of your audiences are likely analytical thinkers. Keep their attention, "cut to the chase", allow time to digest your message and questions, and gain their approval.

- **Allow for questions and discussion:** Ask for questions and comments. Solicit the input of the audience and value their feedback. Feedback is a gift. This will help you gain credibility with the conceptual thinkers who want to ensure all potential for the proposal is uncovered. It will also allow all other stakeholders to share their thoughts and provide input as well.

- **STP, PSB, and More:** Use the templates we shared in Chapter 8. They work! Incorporate your top value propositions into your presentation to satisfy the "WII-FM" needs of the audience.

Figures 9.5 and 9.6 are examples that show you how to satisfy the needs of a diverse audience where all thinking styles are potentially present. We illustrate the PSB and STP models as they are most widely used.

Figure 9.5 PSB Example

Objective: Decrease Time Required to Meet Product Shipments to Key Partners and Customers through a Process Improvement Project		
Presentation Component	**Component Breakout**	**Who is Motivated?**
Problem: We are not meeting our Service Level Agreement (SLA) Commitments.	• Shipment time averages 6 days. SLA promises a 4 day shipment time. • Customer/partner complaints are increasing. • Employees are frustrated by the situation and number of complaints.	• Logical, objective, and practical explanation of SLA issue satisfies analytical and structural thinkers. • Impact on customer and employee satisfies analytical thinker. Frustration levels resonate with the social thinker who empathizes with the employees.
Solution: Apply DMAIC model to reduce time to ship. (Define, Measure, Analyze, Improve, Control)	• **Step 1:** Map processes. Define and Measure "As Is". Improve teamwork. • **Step 2:** Analyze. Look for variations and improvement opportunities. • **Step 3:** Implement and Control the "To Be" process.	• Logical and efficient step- by-step approach satisfies analytical and structural thinkers. Teamwork appeals to social thinker. • Analysis and opportunities motivate conceptual thinkers. • Implementation and control satisfies analytical and structural thinker expectations.
Benefits: 1. Reduce time to ship. Reduce resource utilization. 2. Improve CSAT. 3. Improve employee satisfaction and reduce turnover rates.	• Time savings, cost reductions, and improved productivity. • Reduction of complaints, higher CSAT, and future improvement opportunities. • Increased employee morale and satisfaction. Reduced turnover.	• Benefits are logical, data oriented (analytical), practical and predictable (structural), fits the big picture need of the company and looks into the future (conceptual), is empathetic for customers and employees, and advocates improved conditions (social).

Figure 9.6 STP Example

Objective: Increase Market Share and Reduce Downward Sales Trends by Expediting Launch of the New DEF Product.		
Presentation Component	**Component Breakout**	**Who is Motivated?**
Situation: Market share for our primary product dropped in the last quarter. Sales are down.	• Market share dropped from 18.3% to 15.2%. • Sales are down by $320,000 as compared to last year. • The DEF product is a replacement. It is six months from launching.	• The Situation keys on data and metrics. Have the proof. • Analytical thinkers will react positively if data is accurate. Structural thinkers will appreciate the practicality of the situation.
Target: Increase market share and sales by expediting DEF product. Exceed competition's features.	• Market research projects increased market share of more than 20% for DEF product. • Conservative estimates project sales increases of at least 5%, and higher commissions for our sales team. • We can meet and beat the competition with launch in four months.	• Data and rational objectives keep the interest of the analytical thinker. Orderly approach works for the structural thinker. • Conceptual thinker is captured by the new ideas and possibilities for the new product. • The benefits to the sales team will provide advocacy from the social thinker.
Proposal& Benefits: 1. Accelerate DEF product development and launch. 2. Market the next generation product. 3. Train our team.	• Accelerate DEF development—regain sales and market share. • Begin marketing campaign. Challenge our team to think of marketing themes— have fun with it. • Institute training program for team—get ready to launch.	• Proposal and benefits motivate all four thinking types as in the case of the PSB example. There is a logical plan (analytical), methodical and practical approach (structural), new ideas (conceptual), and team involvement (social).

Step 4: Remotivating the Audience—Reinforcing the "Why"

Audiences generally remember the first and last things they hear. Take advantage of this fact, and don't end your presentation abruptly. An age old formula for effective presentations we shared earlier is, "Tell them what you will talk about, stay within the subject when you speak, and end with a summary of what you talked about." The Remotivation Step is the summary of what you just talked about, and an opportunity to make a strong final impression.

- Try to select the most compelling value proposition your Business Case offers and share it. People learn from repetition. Don't be reluctant to reiterate a key value proposition you shared earlier.

- Gauge your audience. What areas of your presentation prompted the most discussion and agreement? This may be a great point to reiterate for your final push toward approval.

- Short testimonials are also very effective as remotivators. Ask a key stakeholder with credibility that supports your Business Case to share a reason why they feel approval is necessary. Optimally, this stakeholder should be a customer or user impacted by what you propose. External stakeholders are often given more consideration than internal stakeholders. It is human nature to be courteous to someone "outside" of the immediate family.

- Do not be "long-winded." Your Remotivation step should take no longer than 30 seconds to one minute. Don't be like the salesman who talks too long, provides too many details, and loses the sale.

- You may sense that some stakeholders are still not convinced. If this is the case, make a pledge to work with other stakeholders to refine the proposal during the project planning stage to incorporate considerations brought up during the presentation. Be flexible. Preliminary concurrence to take the next step is a form of a win.

Step 5: Conclusion and Final Steps—Sharing the "Ask"

The last step in the effective presentation process is often overlooked or handled poorly. This is your "Ask." We present our thoughts and ideas to receive feedback. Feedback requirements can be explained using the "PIE" model. Determine the required level of commitment you need from the audience to move the idea forward.

- **P - Persuade:** Most Business Cases attempt to persuade decision makers to accept a proposal. Don't leave without a decision.

- **I - Inform:** Some Business Cases inform. Your Business Case may be in response to a problem management asked you to address, and a solution you were tasked to implement. In this case, use the presentation to inform decision makers of your plan to move forward to the project stage. This is an informative presentation with a purpose to attain validation that everyone is "on the same page."

- **E – Entertain:** Most Business Cases do not seek to entertain the audience. However, a little personality goes a long way in achieving your objectives to persuade and inform. Be yourself, say hello, smile, and say thank you.

Ask for what you want: There are three potential responses to a Business Case. One is yes—you were successful. Yes may be conditional approval to take the next steps. However, that is still a yes! The second is no—ask if there is anything you can provide above and beyond what you presented to change the decision. Third is a request for more information. If that is the case, react quickly while the attention is highest.

Outline next steps: Define your plan for next steps and gain concurrence from the audience that they are committed to support the proposal. As a rule, if you do not define next steps, there will probably be no next steps!

Responding to Questions

You will likely receive some questions during your Business Case presentation. Look upon these questions as an opportunity to "seal the deal." Here are some considerations to remember when questions are asked.

- **Be an active listener:** Listen to the entire question. Don't be afraid to pause for a second to think about a response. Active listening pays dividends. If you need to buy some additional time, paraphrase the question in your words to ensure you truly understand what is being asked. Always respond to the question that was asked. Don't go off on a tangent, and don't go on and on and on! We discussed the salesman who talked so much he lost the sale? Don't fall into that trap.

- **Provide accurate responses:** Try to answer each question as accurately as possible. If you don't know an answer, be honest and respectfully take a "rain check" on the response. Don't guess, and by all means, don't lie. Your credibility is on the line. If possible, invite supporters and Subject Matter Experts (SME) to the presentation and ask them to respond to questions pertinent to their areas of expertise.

- **Anticipate Difficult Questions:** Plan ahead and try to put yourself in the shoes of the audience. Try to anticipate the questions they have ahead of time, and plan responses before the formal presentation. The recommendation to have SMEs available holds true here. In addition, review our overview of the four thinking attributes we discussed in the Emergenetics section. This may give you an indication of the type of questions a particular decision maker may ask.

- **Devil's Advocate Approach:** The Devil's Advocate approach is effective if you think some stakeholders may ask questions in an effort to convince decision makers to disapprove your Business Case. Ask your team members and colleagues to review your Business Case and think of any reasons not to approve the proposal. Build around these objections, anticipate questions, and plan responses ahead of time.

- **Prepare and Rehearse:** There is no substitute for practice. Find a friend, colleague, or team member and walk through your Business Case presentation. Ask the listener to provide constructive feedback, and promise to do the same for them in the future.

- **Acknowledge Questioner Experience:** Consider the experience of the individual asking a question. If a new stakeholder asks a question, provide a quick overview that will not waste time and bore the remainder of the audience. You may even offer to provide background information after the presentation. On the other hand, if an experienced stakeholder asks a question, respond in kind. Provide the level of information he or she is seeking, and try to clarify the response for the general audience as much as possible. If the response will take too much time, put it in the "Parking Lot." Caution—there may be times when you receive a question that is complex and beyond your knowledge level. If that is the case, offer to work with the questioner off-line, or ask them what they think. A great strategy is to say, "You are an acknowledged expert in this area. I'd be gratified to hear your response to this question. Please share your insight."

- **Use proven questioning techniques:** Reversing, redirecting, and rephrasing are three effective precision questioning techniques. You may need to use these techniques during your Business Case presentation.

  o **Reversing**: Reversing a question is an attempt to remove a negative cast and turn it positive. Negative questions can lead to more negativism unless you are able to reverse the trend. For example, a decision maker may ask, "Why did the last version of this product lose so much money?" You can turn that around by stating, "We are confident we've addressed issues in our previous version to the point where the new product upgrade we are proposing will exceed current sales forecasts."

o **Rephrasing:** You may want to rephrase a question to allow for an easier response. In some cases, a decision maker may pose a long, drawn-out question that has many sub points. Try to rephrase the question in a simpler form and provide a response. Ask for validation that you addressed the main point of the question. If not, the decision maker will likely provide a more defined question the second time around.

o **Redirecting:** You may want to redirect a question that is beyond your scope of understanding to an SME. Anticipate questions you may receive before the presentation, and have the right people available to provide a response on your behalf.

- **Plant questions:** It may be beneficial to ask some key stakeholders or supporters of your Business Case to begin the question and answer period with a "safe" question that is easy to respond to, and supports your Business Case approval or disapproval objectives.

A great Business Case presentation can fall apart during the question and answer session. Plan ahead, anticipate questions, practice responses, and have the right people you need at the presentation to provide support. In most cases, you present a Business Case to gain approval for a proposal. Anticipate questions from stakeholders who advocate the status quo. You need to win them over!

Remember that there may be times when you are presenting a Business Case to get an idea disapproved. Anticipate tough questions from the individual or team that wants their idea to be approved. We are confident many of the tools we've shared in this book will help you win the day.

Dealing with a Tough or Non-Supportive Audience

Your audience for a Business Case presentation may not always be motivated and supportive. Some Business Cases propose difficult objectives, and pose tough choices. This section addresses this situation and provides some guidance we trust will assist you in surviving and succeeding.

- **Be Empathetic:** Audiences can be tough when there is a pain point impacting their environment. Find the pain, acknowledge the pain, and address it. If there is anger, acknowledge that as well. An angry person needs to acknowledge their feelings before they can move past them. Don't try to convince the audience that they are wrong for feeling the way they do. Sometimes even a well-timed smile can help ease the tensions. Empathy works!

- **Smoothing:** There are times when emotions may run high during the presentation. Smoothing is a conflict management technique that attempts to find a foundational point of agreement for all stakeholders that can be built upon. For example, "We all agree that the staffing cut recommendations are painful. However, can everyone agree that we need to take action to downsize our operations in these difficult economic times to survive?"

- **Practice and Plan:** The tougher the audience, the more practice you need. Do your homework. Anticipate audience frustration, and plan ahead on how to effectively deal with it. If possible, find someone who has shared a similar experience, and consider their thoughts on how to best proceed and succeed.

- **Deliver Effectively:** Actual delivery is almost a performing art. There are a few tactics that have proven to be positive.

  o Move towards the audience in a non-confronting manner. Show no fear. If standing, step toward the person. Be careful to avoid entering their social zone. In addition, be calm and empathetic as you move.

o   If sitting, lean towards the audience. This shows that you are willing to engage in a "lively discussion" of the subject. In addition, it shows that you aren't afraid to address a tough issue, or respond to a difficult question.

- **Don't tie names to negatives**: Avoid linking negative emotions to an individual. This action may invoke strong defensive reactions and make matters worse. Sometimes frustrated stakeholders play the "blame game." Remember to keep the focus on the issue or proposal, not the stakeholders who may or may not have caused the problem.

- **Don't repeat negatives**: If you are asked, "So why was product XYZ launched with so many problems?" Your answer should not include the words "Product XYZ was launched with so many problems because…" Instead answer, "We added a great amount of new functionality to the new product which resulted in some issues that caught us by surprise. We are confident we have addressed those issues in this new proposal."

- **Stay Cool**: Avoid emotional outbursts. Take a deep breath, and avoid getting heated over a debate. Buy yourself some time by restating the question, and asking for more details. Try to look beyond the immediate question, and try to determine what is behind the question. Determine the root cause and address the issue. Don't get caught up in the emotion.

- **Appeal to Fairness**: Asking for fairness will often result in the stakeholder toning down their question. A statement such as, "I know we are all frustrated. Can I ask you to please concentrate on how we can reduce our frustration by coming up with the best decision possible under the circumstances. I need your help!"

Tough audiences are sometimes a reality. Stay focused on the issues, empathize with the stakeholders, and find a common point of reference. You may be able to turn a negative situation into an eventual win for the organization.

Using Voice, Gestures, and Body Language Effectively

Your presentation style can oftentimes influence chances for success or failure. Here are some presentation tips to consider as you present your Business Case. Give yourself every opportunity to succeed.

Using Your Voice Effectively

Your voice is a tool you should learn to use effectively. Here are some tips to improve your voice effectiveness.

- **Volume:** Speak to be heard. Avoid shouting or whispering. Judge the room, number of people, and other logistics. If possible, go to where you are presenting with an associate and practice beforehand.

- **Pace:** Try to speak at a normal rate. Don't rush or intentionally try to slow down for the audience. Normal speaking is 120 words per minute. Listeners can normally follow four to five times the pace of your speech. The exception to this rule is when you present in an international environment where your primary language may not be the primary language of the audience. You may want to adjust your pace downward when this is the case.

- **Articulation:** Take your time, and pronounce words correctly. Use words that are familiar to the audience, and avoid acronyms and jargon that may confuse them and lead to a lack of comprehension. Be aware of regional word variations, and use standard language.

- **Intonation:** Use pitch to your advantage. Vary your delivery approach to match the subject matter. Avoid the "monotone" approach. Intonation can be used to stress words, concepts, or show your passion for your Business Case proposal.

- **Stress:** Emphasize key words when you need to. Know the most important points, and relay that importance. Stressing words in conjunction with positive gestures can be a winning one-two combination.

- **Pause:** The pause button works well at times! Pause when you want a thought to sink in. The pause is mandatory after a rhetorical question. You want the point you are trying to make truly resonate and stick.

- **"KISS":** Remember that often times "less is more!" We've said it before and we'll say it again--don't oversell your Business Case. Give the audience adequate levels of information to make a decision. If they have questions, they will ask you for more details. "Keep it Short and Sweet."

- **Choice of Words:** Be careful with words when presenting. Slang and off-color words are potentially "explosive." Attempts at joking can doom you to failure if the words offend. Avoid discussing politics, religion, and any other subjects not pertinent to your Business Case proposal.

- **Avoid "Filler Words" Usage:** Filler words are those verbal pauses and missteps like "Um and Ah", or thrown in words such as "Ya Know or Like." Be aware of your potential to use filler words and try to avoid them. Familiarity and confidence in your materials generally result in the use of fewer filler words. Practice makes perfect!

Gestures

The way you use your hands or body can assist or detract from the impact of your presentation. Gestures help your audience follow your presentation, add life to your message, and stress points you want to make. Here are some tips to remember.

- **Gestures:** Gestures stress, demonstrate or compliment your presentation. In addition, they can act as a means to create a picture to accompany your words.

- **Practice:** Practice in advance. One of the most common errors is to force the use of gestures that do not fit the presentation. Use gestures to fit the space. Use hands, shoulders, elbows, etc.

- **The "Globe":** A common teaching technique for new presenters is the "holding the globe" method. Hold your hands in front of you as you would do so to hold a globe. Don't drop it. Allow your natural enthusiasm and energy to naturally move your hands in a way that compliments your words.

- **Hands:** Try to keep your hands from going to the wrong places. Hands in pockets, wringing of hands, playing with jewelry, glasses, etc. are quite distracting to the audience. People will notice your mannerisms and lose focus of the presentation.

Body Language

Effective use of body language also has an impact on presentation effectiveness. The Project Management Institute states that body language is 55% of what you communicate, and your words are only 45%. Here are some keys to success.

- **Personal Space:** Watch "personal" space. This can vary from country to country. Try not to get too close to people. This makes them feel uncomfortable. Avoid touching people unless you are confident your actions will be accepted and are pertinent to the presentation. Handshakes are of course an exception to this rule.

- **Posture:** Watch your posture – be alert and erect. Avoid "slouching" or stiffness. Avoid hiding behind the podium, or leaning against an object. Show your passion and excitement. Don't give the audience the impression that you lack motivation and are simply going through the motions.

- **Voiceless Signals**: Use "voiceless" signals when necessary or practical. A smile, head nod, etc. can convey both your thoughts and your personality far better than words. A well-timed smile may change a presentation from negative to positive in an instant.

- **Movement:** Don't be a static presenter. Don't be afraid to take a few steps in any direction. There are two benefits. First, it allows the audience to move their eyes. Staring at a fixed object can be almost hypnotic. You don't want to chance putting your audiences in a mental state where they really can't hear a word you are saying. Movement also helps control your nerves. Every presenter has some anxiety prior to presenting. I like to call this anxiety "butterflies." Movement can help relax you, remove your anxiety, and allow those butterflies to "fly in formation!"

Facial Expressions

Your facial expressions are the most revealing form of non-verbal communication you can share with an audience. You need to make sure the message you convey is positive and upbeat. Here are some points to remember:

- **Eyes:** "The eye is the light of the body."[7] Your eyes can show confidence, passion, empathy, etc. Avoid rolling your eyes or ignoring the audience. Strive for eye contact with every member, look into the eyes of the individual you are addressing, and think kindness and empathy.

- **Smile:** Smile and be personable. Show the audience that you are a human being and not a target. This will help you and others to relax. It also helps to break the ice when the audience is not familiar with one another.

- **Lips:** The lips speak when they are silent. Use pauses and variations in pace to your advantage. Avoid tightening your lips. Verbalize negative messages in a way where they may not want to hear your words, but understand and accept your meaning.

Effective Business Case Presentation Techniques: Other Keys

There are some additional keys to success worth sharing before we close out this chapter. Here is a list to consider when presenting your Business Case.

- **Practice the Presentation:** You have heard the term, "Practice makes perfect." Practice your presentation with associates and peers you can trust. Gain feedback. It is best to make mistakes during the practice session you can address prior to the actual presentation.

- **Dress for Success:** Try to determine the "dress code" for the day and blend in. You will look out of place in a three-piece suit if everyone else is in casual clothing. On the other hand, you will be noticed if everyone is wearing business casual, and you walk into the room in shorts and sandals.

---

[7] *How to be a Great Communicator*, Qubein

- **Use Definitive Terms:** Avoid terms such as "we think, maybe, could, and should." Strive to use terminology that instills confidence such as "we know, will, can, etc." The words you choose reflect the courage and conviction of you and your team.

- **Own the Space:** You are presenting. Take control of the environment. Move around the room in a reasonable fashion. Move toward people. Show confidence.

- **Be Yourself:** The best presenter is you. Don't try to be someone you are not. The most authentic presentation is one that reflects the presenter's true personality and passion.

- **Be Passionate:** Show excitement for what you propose. Try to find other stakeholders willing to share their passion as well during the actual presentation.

- **Use Names:** If possible, mention people in the audience by name in a positive manner. People love to hear their names. For example, "Mr. Spence has mentioned on numerous occasions the importance of ensuring our CSAT scores remain high." Mr. Spence will probably nod, smile, and provide support to your value proposition.

- **Talk to Your Slides:** Use your slides as a guide. Try to avoid reading them. If need be, make some note cards you can hold that define key points. It is perfectly acceptable to periodically glance at your notes to ensure you stay on track. Try to be as extemporaneous as possible.

Effective Business Case Presentation Techniques Summary

This concludes our overview of presentation techniques. Remember the five-step approach we shared. It works. In addition, review the tips on answering questions, dealing with tough audiences, and our section on using voice, gestures, and body language effectively. Figure 9.7 summarizes many of the points made in this chapter in the form of a checklist you can use to gauge your readiness to present.

Figure 9.7 Business Case Presentation Readiness Checklist

Consideration	Ready: Yes or No?
Time: Did I develop my presentation to meet time requirements? Do I have an elevator speech "just in case?"	
Organization: Did I organize my presentation in a manner that supports my objectives?	
Brevity: Am I over selling? Does every piece of information I plan to share have a purpose?	
Adaptability: Do I have a plan to adapt to audience questions, hostility toward the objective, etc.?	
Support: Do I have supporting information for all key facts, figures, etc.?	
Questions: Do I know the most likely questions? Have I practiced responses?	
Credibility: Do I need to establish credibility as a knowledgeable presenter? If so, how can I establish credibility quickly?	
Audience: Do I know my audience? Have I adapted my presentation to capture support from multiple thinking styles?	
Meeting Before the Meeting: Should I consider a pre-meeting to discuss aspects of the Business Case with key stakeholders?	
Apply the Grease: Are there any key stakeholders I should solicit support from before the presentation?	
Devil's Advocate: Will my proposal result in negative responses? Is a Devil's Advocate approach warranted?	
Team Composition: Who needs to be part of the presentation team? Should I assign roles to others for support?	

We now provide a chapter for a very special group of visionaries. Chapter 10 discusses variations to what we have shared to this point, and provides secrets of success for the Social Entrepreneurs of the world.

Chapter 9 "Food for Thought"

Part I:

Use the template below to plan your five-step Business Case presentation. Share your plan with an associate for validation.

Step	Your Plan
Attention: How will I gain the audience's attention?	
Motivation: How can I motivate the audience to listen?	
Body: Which presentation template should I use? What are the key points?	
Remotivation: What is the key thought I want to leave the audience with?	
Close: What will I ask for?	

Part II:

Use the template below to plan ahead for other factors that will impact your presentation.

Consideration	Notes
Questions: What are potential questions that may be asked? What is the best response?	
Audience: Who is my audience? Are they receptive, hostile, or neutral? What is my plan? Do I know their thinking attributes?	
Other Factors: What are the presentation logistics? What do I need to concentrate on to be effective?	

My Notes:

Chapter 10: The Social Entrepreneurship Business Case

Social Entrepreneurship[8] ventures are on the increase. A Social Entrepreneur recognizes a social problem, and uses sound business practices to organize, create and manage a venture to achieve social change. This goal is referred to as a Social Venture. Social Entrepreneurs are agents of change.

While a Business Entrepreneur typically measures performance in profit and return, a Social Entrepreneur focuses on creating social capital. Thus, the main aim of Social Entrepreneurship is to further social and environmental goals. Social Entrepreneurs are most commonly associated with the voluntary and not-for-profit sectors, but this doesn't rule out making a profit. Some Social Ventures are actually created as for-profit corporations.

Social Entrepreneurs need to develop a compelling Business Case and a sound Business Plan to sell their ventures to supporters, contributors, potential recipients of their services, and more. This chapter provides some guidance for the Social Entrepreneur who has an idea to achieve a needed change for the betterment of many, and needs guidance to achieve their goals. We follow the same step-by-step process shared throughout this book up to this point.

Step 1: Define Objectives

A traditional Business Case is generally developed to propose an idea to support corporate or organizational goals and objectives. A "Business Case for Life Decisions" is accomplished to develop an individualized improvement plan. We discuss this Business Case iteration in the next chapter.

A Business Case to support a Social Entrepreneurship idea is often much broader. Your idea can impact a small segment of society, or reach across vast distances, cultures, and boundaries. The potential to make a difference is great. As such, you need to refine and define your objectives in a manner that truly shows what you want to accomplish, where you want to accomplish it, and who will benefit. You need a solid and compelling objective! Here are some tips to remember.

---

[8] www.Wikipedi.com

a. **What is Your Specific Objective:** You need to be able to define the specific social issue you want to address in terms that are accurate, brief, and concise. A volunteer's interpretation of your objective should match that of a potential donor or financial investor. Develop your objective using the action-result methodology we shared in Chapter 2. Start with your high-level objective, and break down your proposed venture into easy to understand, smaller, and manageable objectives. The longer it takes for a stakeholder to determine what you want to do, the lower the chances of successfully selling your proposal. Breaking down your idea into smaller sub-sections allows a potential supporter to see study the big picture of what you are proposing. It also allows decision makers to pick and choose the segments they would most like to support.

b. **Mission and Vision Statement:** Every Social Entrepreneur should develop a compelling Mission and Vision Statement to supplement their objective. The Mission Statement should address how you plan to create and sustain social value. We previously referenced Jim Collin's book, *Good to Great*. He states that the best vision shows your ultimate Big Hairy Audacious Goal (BHAG), and the value proposition you offer. Think big! A great Mission and Vision Statement acknowledge the need to move a venture forward carefully. However, it also acknowledges the opportunities on the horizon as well. We will feature an example of a solid Mission Statement at the end of this section.

c. **Segmentation: Who and Where:** Who will your proposal help, and where are these recipients located. Many Social Ventures try to do too much, too soon. Try to define and confine the location and population segment you want to help when you begin. Use this segment as a proof of concept before you try to expand. This will reduce costs, and help you gain credibility. Investors and supporters love a proven winner. This rule may not be true for all ventures. However, it holds true for the vast majority of ideas. One of the major reasons ideas fail is because the Social Entrepreneur tries to scale and expand too quickly.

d. **Time Phasing-When:** When will you implement your proposal? Is there a plan to launch your venture? These will be up-front questions you receive from many stakeholders. Refer to the WBS example we shared in Chapter 6; Figure 6.3. This model may help you respond.

e. **Problem Support:** Make sure you have documented support that acknowledges the validity of the problem you want to solve. Great sources of support you can share are testimonials from people who your proposal will assist. In addition, quotes, articles, reports, etc. from credible sources are also keys to success. Try to find support for the value of solving the problem as well. How will solving the problem help the people impacted by your solution, the environment, economy, key stakeholders, etc.

f. **Multi-Media Support:** Videos, pictures, and documentaries that substantiate your objective can also play a key role in capturing attention and support for your objective. Ensure whatever media you use is authentic, accurate, and relates to the problem you are proposing to solve.

Mission Statement Example

Seth Goldman is the co-founder of a company named Honest Tea ®. Seth graciously consented to allowing me to use his Mission Statement as an example for other Social Entrepreneurs to follow. Here is a copy of Honest Tea's Mission Statement from their website[9].

"MISSION STATEMENT"

"Honest Tea creates and promotes delicious, truly healthy, organic beverages. We strive to grow with the same honesty we use to craft our products, with sustainability and great taste for all. "

---

[9] www.honesttea.com

"ASPIRATIONS FOR CORPORATE SOCIAL RESPONSIBILITY (CSR)"

"We will never claim to be a perfect company, but we will address difficult issues and strive to be honest about our ability or inability to resolve them. We will strive to work with our suppliers to promote higher standards. We value diversity in the workplace and intend to become a visible presence in the communities where our products are sold. When presented with a purchasing decision between two financially comparable alternatives, we will attempt to choose the option that better addresses the needs of economically disadvantaged communities.

A commitment to social responsibility is central to Honest Tea's identity and purpose. The company strives for authenticity, integrity and purity, in our products and in the way we do business. In addition to creating a healthy alternative beverage with a lot less sugar than most bottled drinks, Honest Tea seeks to create honest relationships with our employees, suppliers, customers and with the communities in which we do business. "

What Can We Learn from Honest Tea?

Honest Tea summarizes the value proposition of its Social Venture well through a two-step approach. Their Mission Statement is short and to the point. They supplement their Mission Statement with their "Aspirations for Corporate Social Responsibility (CSR)" statement. Note how Honest Tea provides a value proposition in a short three paragraphs that tracks to all four components of the Balanced Scorecard model.

- **Mission Statement:** The Mission Statement shares the fact that Honest Tea has a great product. This definitely is a financial perspective plus. It discusses the positive impact of its organic product to society—a key to success to satisfy the diverse needs of a worldwide customer base. This satisfies the customer perspective. They also share how their processes are built to sustain and grow the corporation. This satisfies the process perspective. There is also a statement of the importance of honesty to operations. This is a key employee perspective match!

- **Aspirations for Corporate Social Responsibility (CSR):** We discussed the "KISS" principle earlier. Less is more—"Keep it Short and Sweet." Honest Tea shares two key paragraphs on Social Responsibility, and doesn't waste a word!

  - **Address the Difficult Issues:** Honest Tea recognizes that the corporate environment is a moving target. They show a willingness to listen to customers, use the creativity of their employees, and improve processes to move forward.

  - **Higher Standards:** Honest Tea is not happy with the status quo. They are aiming to move relationships and operations with suppliers to the next level.

  - **Diversity:** Honest Tea publicly recognizes talents that a diverse group of stakeholders bring to an organization, and makes a commitment to embrace them.

  - **Help the Disadvantaged:** A huge value proposition gained from a successful Social Entrepreneurship venture is to not only help society, but change the world environment for the better. Honest Tea pledges to help those who need it the most. They will choose to support the suppliers with the greatest need, even if that does not result in the greatest Return on Investment!

  - **Product and Business Specifics:** Honest Tea strives for authenticity, integrity and purity in both product development and operations. They also aspire to provide a healthy product that addresses a current societal issue—making the right decisions that impact health, obesity, sugar consumption, etc.

  - **Honesty:** Honest Tea strives to live up to its name in all things they do. They share a compelling pledge to all.

Honest Tea defines its objectives as a Social Entrepreneurship through its Mission Statement and CSR Statement. This is a superb example for aspiring Social Entrepreneurs to follow. We will revisit Honest Tea later in this chapter.

Step 2: Define the Value Proposition

The Balanced Scorecard model discussed in Chapter 3 can be used by the Social Entrepreneur to identify potential value propositions. There are a number of additional considerations you should consider as well. Let's revisit the four perspectives of the Balanced Scorecard from a Social Entrepreneurship standpoint.

1. **Financial Perspective:** How will you finance your venture?

    a. **Sustain and Grow:** How will you bring in operating dollars? What product or service value can you offer? How can you sustain the operations? What are your plans to grow? These are key questions you need to address to gain financial support. Don't be afraid to aim high!

    b. **Donated Funds/Grants:** What value do you offer to those willing to support you through grants and donations? What is the payback in terms of tangibles and intangibles? What is the WII-FM? Supporters want to know.

    c. **Unique Selling Position (USP):** Is there competition? Has anyone tried the type of Social Venture you are proposing before? How are you different than the competitors? How do you stand out? What is your niche? You need to show that what you propose is a step above the rest.

    d. **The Triple Bottom Line:** What are your financial goals? Do you want to accomplish social change? Do you want to earn high profits? Do you want to improve the environment? All three of these goals will require funds. Many Social Entrepreneurs aim to accomplish all three. We introduced Honest Tea in a previous section. Here is a quick case study of how Seth Goldman applied the "Triple Bottom Line" to his Honest Tea business[10]. Seth Goldman founded Honest Tea in 1998 as a means to bridge the gap between drinks that were too sweet and those with little taste[11]. There are never guarantees for future success. However, Honest Tea has sustained and grown since its creation. The future looks bright for Honest Tea.

---

[10] www.En.wikibooks.org
[11] www.honesttea.com

- **High Profits:** Seth has created a successful corporation. The Coca-Cola Corporation recently purchased a 40% stake in Honest Tea worth approximately $43 Million. There is no reason why a Social Venture cannot be profitable. Social Entrepreneurships and profitability are not mutually exclusive.

- **Social Change:** Honest Tea markets their drinks as possessing fewer calories and less sugar than other selections. In addition, Honest Tea claims that almost the entire line of drinks offered is organic. There are many people in the world today who suffer from obesity, health issues, etc. Honest Tea offers a healthier alternative.

- **Change the Environment:** Honest Tea believes that organic production leads to fewer toxins being placed in water, land, and people's bodies. In addition, Honest Tea strives to create relationships with suppliers and partners in some of the poorest nations on the planet. This creates wealth where it is needed the most, and greatly contributes to our environment.

e. **Scalability:** How do you plan to scale and expand your footprint? Will you have the funds to eliminate pain on a widespread basis, or even change the overall environment? Is there potential to reach out to new segments, add new services, take your venture to the next level, etc. The ability to launch a basic venture that can be scaled is a Critical Success Factor in the minds of potential supporters.

f. **Exit Strategy for Investors:** How can investors potentially get their money back with fair Return on Investment? What is your payback strategy? A reality is that supporters and investors require some Return on Investment. This includes both intangible and tangible returns. You need to show the value in both areas.

2. **Internal Business or Process Perspective:** How will your plan come together? How will your venture improve the current economic situation? What is your vision of "success?" This key perspective addresses these questions.

   a. **Economic/Environmental Improvement:** How will your venture improve the environment? What is the impact if we do nothing? How is the current environment today, and how will you change it for the better? Show how the "As Is" state is not a satisfactory solution.

   b. **Flexibility and Openness to Learn:** Is your venture open to new ideas and modifications. Do you have a "one size fits all" solution, or one that is flexible? Many potential partners will offer ideas. Listen carefully and adopt the ones that make sense.

   c. **Connections:** What connections do you have that will help pave the way for success? Internal connections and external connections can be of great assistance in terms of identifying key sources of support, networking, overcoming bureaucracy, etc. Local connections in the environment where your Social Venture will "reside" are a Critical Success Factor.

   d. **Politics:** Are there internal or external political factors you need to address? How will you position your Social Venture to overcome them? Political factors are risks. You need a plan to work through them.

   e. **Technology:** How will you use technology to your advantage? What is your overall technical architecture plan? Technology can lead to both opportunities and threats. Show the opportunities you envision.

   f. **Competition:** Who is the competition? What is your competitive advantage? Do you have a Unique Selling Position (USP)? Remember, you need to sell your idea as, "better than the rest!"

2. **Employee or Innovation and Learning Perspective:** What considerations matter for your employees and volunteers? You must address this perspective as well.

   a. **Team:** Who is your team? Do you have the level of passion and expertise required to succeed? Are there limitations? Are there competent and skilled human resources available in the environment where you plan to launch your Social Venture? If so, how will you take advantage of opportunities and overcome any potential limitations?

   b. **Cultural Liaison:** Do you have team members who can act as cultural liaison(s) and forge relationships you will need to be successful? Is there a special team member who can coach and mentor you on cultural and environmental realities? Identification of cultural liaison(s) eases the fears of potential supporters.

   c. **Employee Motivation:** How will you recruit, motivate, and retain employees? How will you sell the value of working for your Social Venture to potential recruits? What are the tangible and intangible benefits employees can count on that will sell them on your idea?

   d. **Volunteer Motivation:** Will you need volunteers? How can you sell volunteers on the benefits of supporting your venture? What makes you stand out from a volunteer standpoint? Ensure you have a plan to solicit volunteers if required in all environments impacted by your venture.

   e. **Training:** How will you train employees and volunteers to serve? Will employees and volunteers see value in this training opportunity? Will working with you allow employees and volunteers to grow? Ensure training, costs, timeframes, etc. considerations are addressed.

3. **Customer Perspective:** Who are the people will you serve? What is the customer's perspective? Describe and address the segment(s) of the population your venture will impact.

    a. **Adoption:** Are there potential resistance issues? Do the people you want to serve want to be helped? How will you reach out to your potential customers and motivate them to be part of your Social Venture? Do you have a plan to overcome potential resistance? Testimonials from prospective customers validating your idea can be a huge plus.

    b. **Variations:** Are you able to support a variety of special circumstances? Will your venture serve the diverse needs of your customer base? This tracks back to the scalability goals we discussed previously. Show how your Social Venture is not a "one size fits all" operation.

    c. **Values:** How do your values match the values of your partners and customers? Show how the values that will drive your Social Venture integrate with all levels of stakeholders whose support you need to enlist.

Step 3: Define Costs and Benefits

The Social Entrepreneur must pay special attention to costs and benefits. Most potential investors and donors want to ensure the Social Venture can sustain itself for the long term. In addition, donors, grant providers, and investment institutions are often very particular about where the funds they provide are spent. You need to be able to show investors and donors that you have a solid plan that will ensure their needs and desires are met.

Sources and Uses of Cash

Figure 10.1 shows an abbreviated Cash Flow Diagram you should consider duplicating. Key features include costs, benefits, and sources of cash. A Cash Flow Diagram can be time-phased by months, quarters, halves, or years. Develop the Cash Flow Diagram that best suits the needs of your Social Venture, and satisfies the desires of key stakeholders involved in the Cash Flow Cycle.

Figure 10.1 Cash Flow Diagram: Uses and Sources of Cash

	Business Case Financials Illustration 10					
	Uses ($) and Sources $ of Cash					
Cash Flow	H1 (6 mo.)	H2 (12 mo.)	H1 (18 mo.)	H2 (24 mo.)	SOURCE	Sub-Total
Furniture	-$1,500	-$3,500	$0	$0	Donor A	($5,000)
AV Equipment		-$3,750		-$1,250	Donor B	($5,000)
Computers	-$4,500	-$800			Bank	($5,300)
Web Support	-$3,000	-$500	-$500	-$500	Operations	($4,500)
Lease Costs	-$9,000	-$9,000	-$9,000	-$9,000	Multiple	($36,000)
Donations	$5,000				Donor A	$5,000
Donations		$5,000			Donor B	$5,000
Income 1	$30,000				Loan	$30,000
Income 2		$15,000			Grant	$15,000
Income 3			$200	$600	Paintings	$800
Total	$17,000	$2,450	-$9,300	-$10,150		$0

- This example shows sources and uses of cash over a two-year period. Totals are shown using a half year (H1, H2, etc.) methodology.

- In this example, we assume Donor "A" provided funds for a furniture purchase. It is important to show how those funds were indeed used to purchase furniture. Donor "B" provided funds for Audio-Visual (AV) equipment. Show how these funds were allocated accordingly.

- Uses and sources of cash should be balanced. Most investors understand that you will be operating in "the red" initially. Strive to show how eventually your Social Venture will be able to sustain itself in the long term.

Pro-Forma Income Statement: Five-Year Plan

Many investors want to see a Five-Year Plan before investing. Their objective is to ensure your venture is sustainable over the long-term. In addition, they want to see where they potentially will fit into the plan. Figure 10.2 provides an example of a Pro-Forma Income Statement which covers a five-year period.

Figure 10.2 Pro-Forma Income Statement Example

PRO Forma Income Statement					
Consideration	**Year 1**	**Year 2**	**Year 3**	**Year 4**	**Year 5**
Beginning Cash Balance	$100,000	$28,408	$23,147	$19,512	$28,771
Total Sales	$20,000	$45,000	$60,000	$75,000	$80,000
Total Donations	$15,000	$35,000	$40,000	$50,000	$50,000
Commissions	$0	$5,000	$8,000	$12,000	$15,000
Grants	$15,000	$15,000	$0	$0	$0
Interest Income	$0	$0	$0	$0	$200
Investment Income	$0	$0	$0	$0	$500
Depreciation Advantage (Value x Tax)	$200	$200	$200	$400	$400
Total Cash Receipts	**$150,200**	**$128,608**	**$131,347**	**$156,912**	**$174,871**
Salaries & Labor	$35,000	$35,000	$38,000	$40,000	$50,000
Donations	$5,000	$8,000	$12,000	$15,000	$20,000
Advertising	$3,000	$3,000	$2,500	$2,500	$2,500
Marketing Research	$3,000	$0	$0	$0	$0
Training	$2,000	$2,000	$2,000	$2,000	$2,000
Travel	$1,500	$1,500	$1,500	$1,500	$1,500
Loan Repayment	$12,000	$12,000	$12,000	$12,000	$12,000
Consulting	$2,000	$0	$0	$0	$0
Commissions	$0	$0	$0	$0	$0
Cost of Goods-Materials	$20,000	$15,000	$15,000	$20,000	$23,000
Building Buy/Lease	$18,000	$18,000	$18,000	$18,000	$18,000
Equipment: Set-Up & Expand	$9,000	$0	$0	$5,000	$0
Supplies/Materials	$2,000	$2,500	$3,000	$3,500	$4,000
Permits	$0	$0	$0	$0	$0
Patents/Copyrights/Licenses	$25	$0	$0	$0	$0
Total Cash Disbursements	**$112,525**	**$97,000**	**$104,000**	**$119,500**	**$133,000**
Earnings Before Interest & Taxes	$37,675	$31,608	$27,347	$37,412	$41,871
Interest Expenses	$5,500	$5,300	$5,100	$4,900	$4,700
Taxes at 10%	$3,768	$3,161	$2,735	$3,741	$4,187
Net Cash Balance/Plowback	**$28,408**	**$23,147**	**$19,512**	**$28,771**	**$32,984**

Step 4: Define Risks

There are a number of risks that can impact a Social Venture. Figure 10.3 provides a comprehensive Risk Breakdown Structure modified for Social Entrepreneurs. Many of the risks identified are similar to the Risk Breakdown Structure provided in Chapter 5. Some, however, are unique.

Figure 10.3 Social Entrepreneurship Risk Breakdown Structure

RBS Category: Legal/Regulatory	
Risk Event	**Impact**
Legal: Legal and compliance requirements may be difficult to define and quantify.	Potential delays. Potential need for additional resources.
Regulatory: Regulatory factors may be unknown or subject to change.	Potential delays or restarts. Potential reduction of Social Venture scope.

RBS Category: Financial	
Risk Event	**Impact**
Costs: Total costs may be based on assumptions and subject to variations.	Impact on budget, funds phasing, grant and donation requests. Impact on overall project scope and schedules.
Start Up Costs: Costs of permits, business licenses, incentives, etc. may be difficult to determine and quantify.	Additional funding requirements. Potential delays to meet required financial obligations.
Returns: Total returns are based on assumptions and may subject to variations.	Impact on budget, funds phasing, grant and donation requests. Impact on venture sustainment and longevity.
Funding Sources: Sources of funds in doubt, or difficult to finalize.	Impact on budget, funds phasing, grant and donation requests.
Cost Controls: Cost control system may be difficult to define and establish.	Impact on budget, funds tracking and reporting, and funds allocation. Potential Governance issues.
Contingency Funds: Unknowns may impact project costs and returns.	Impact on cost phasing, budgets. Potential cost overruns and stakeholder dissatisfaction.
Funds Requests: Inadequate grant writing and loan proposal expertise may impact funds availability.	Impact on budget, funds phasing, grant and donation requests. Impact on overall project scope and schedules

RBS Category: Project/Solution	
Risk Event	**Impact**
Awareness: Creating awareness of project may be difficult.	Low or delayed acceptance of project. Lack of support, volunteers, employees, etc.
Social Problem/Change Management: May encounter challenges convincing stakeholders social problem is compelling. May encounter resistance to proposed change.	Limited project support, reduced buy-in, lower donations, etc. Slow transition to new process/plan you propose.
Value Proposition: Stakeholders may not prioritize need to address your idea as high priority compared to other proposals.	Low acceptance. Limited funding and donations. Lack of resource support. Reduced volunteer numbers.
Communications Plan: Communication Plan may not serve the needs of stakeholders. May not get information to stakeholders in a timely manner.	Impacts stakeholder accomplishment of project activities. Impacts right information to the right stakeholder in the right quantity at the right time.
Mission and Vision: Mission Statement and Vision may be misunderstood, or fail to capture attention of stakeholders.	Confusion. Low or delayed acceptance of project. Reduced financial support.
Goals and Objectives: Goals and objectives may not motivate stakeholders into action.	Confusion. Low or delayed acceptance of project.
Scope: Objectives may be ambiguous to stakeholders. Venture features and benefits may be misunderstood.	Low acceptance. Limited funding and donations. Lack of resource support. Reduced volunteers.
Measurement: Objectives may be difficult to track and measure.	Difficulty in convincing stakeholders there is value in pursuing the project.
Competition: Other organizations may be attempting similar initiatives.	Supporters may not see value in your project. May misunderstand, or not see, your Unique Sales Position (USP).
Impact on Other Organizations: Proposed solution may impact external organizational processes and business methods.	Resistance to change. Push back. Attempts to sabotage your initiative.
Technology: May not have technological knowledge and expertise needed to implement project.	Delayed schedules, additional resource requirements, and lack of acceptance/buy-in.

RBS Category: Schedule	
Risk Event	**Impact**
Schedule: Potential planned milestones will not be met due to uncertainties.	Stakeholder dissatisfaction. Customer churn. Impact on budget and scope.
Estimating: Schedule estimating techniques may be insufficient to plan effective launch date.	Schedule may require extending. Planned resources may not be sufficient. Project scope may suffer.
Dependencies: May experience difficulty identifying and calculating impact of external, mandatory, and discretionary dependencies. (See Glossary for definitions)	Final schedule may not be realistic. May experience long-term impacts on scope and budget.
Schedule Controls: Schedule control system may be difficult to define and establish.	Impact on schedule, scope, budget, resources, customer satisfaction, and overall project quality.

RBS Category: Cultural/Ethical	
Risk Event	**Impact**
Cultural: May encounter different values and perspectives that impact your vision. Socioeconomic status variances may create issues.	Potential resistance, frustration, or delays. Communications impacts.
Ethics: May encounter those with opposing ethical views.	Potential lost partnerships, reduced benefits to society, dissention, stress, and frustration.
Religious: Donors may object to funding specific religious activities or endeavors.	Reduced donor funding potential. Need to designate funds for specific sources. Need to segregate religious-based activities from other support.

RBS Category: Resources	
Risk Event	**Impact**
Stakeholder Identification: Potential to overlook key stakeholders and not define their roles.	Schedule delays. Resource impacts. Potential legal, compliance, buy-in issues, etc.
Volunteer availability: Limited volunteer availability may become a reality.	Delayed schedules and scope. Need for additional budget. Lowered team morale, esprit de corps. Frustration.
Proper skills: Proper skills may not be available, or required skill sets may be unknown.	Need to add resources and schedule extensions. Reduction in scope possible. Time delays to identify, train, and find skilled team members.
Executive Support: Community and financial institutes may not effectively partner and evangelize your project.	Delays, lack of buy-in, difficulty in finding volunteers and donations. Limited success of the venture.
Management Support: Internal stakeholders may lack the management skills necessary to support the venture.	Delayed schedules. Need for additional budget. Lowered team morale, esprit de corps. Frustration. False starts.
Affiliation: May not know which organizations/stakeholders to network or connect with.	Lost opportunities and increased threats. May impact scope, budget, schedules, etc.
Training: Training plan may not meet needs of internal and external stakeholders.	Stakeholders may not have skills necessary to be both efficient and effective.
Roles and Responsibilities: Stakeholders may not accept assigned roles and responsibilities. Level of commitment may be lacking.	Delayed schedules and scope. Need for additional budget. Lowered team morale, esprit de corps. Frustration. Need for additional change management activities.
Organizational Culture and/or Structure: Your organizational structure or culture may not be compatible with external stakeholder organizations.	False starts. Lost partnerships. Failure to achieve opportunities. Increased communication challenges.
Organizational Stability: Partner organizations may experience changes, reorganizations, responsibility shifts, etc.	Project delays. Scope and budget impact. Need for effective change management. Extensive plan updates.
Motivation: Levels of commitment may be lacking due to poorly defined achievement, affiliation, and empowerment concepts.	Resistance and frustration. Potential churn. Failure to accomplish roles and responsibilities.

Step 5: Provide Supporting Data and Information

The majority of the concepts we addressed in Chapter 6 hold true for the Social Entrepreneur's Business Case. There are a few additional entries you may need to consider.

1. **Governance:** Corporate Governance can be defined as policies and processes to oversee the direction and management of the firm to ensure it fulfills its mandate. Social Ventures need to have a Governance policy that ensures ethical operations, proper use of funds, non-profit status accountability, etc. Some considerations to consider include:

   - Approving the strategic direction and changes to operational principles. Ensuring publication and adherence to a corporate or strategic plan.

   - Ensuring that potential threats and opportunities identified as high priority risks are identified and managed. Refer to Chapter 5. Risks impact the creation and the operations of any venture. Monitoring and controlling risk is an on-going process.

   - Defining a decision-making methodology and ensuring adherence. Ensuring all decisions are consistent with approved operational guidelines.

   - Monitoring performance to ensure planned metrics and measures equal actual results.

   - How will /leadership management be elected? Who is the Board of Directors and what roles do they play? What is the leadership succession plan? How will appointments, training, compensation, etc. be handled?

2. **Sustainment:** We discussed this topic previously. It is worth addressing again. How will the Social Venture sustain operations? What is the step-by-step plan to become self-sustaining over time? Consider products and services that can be produced for profit by the individuals benefitting from your Social Venture. In addition:

   - How will you train the individuals impacted by your Social Venture? How will you equip them to be self-sustaining, and allow them to benefit and grow?

   - What economic benefits will be gained in the environment or region your venture will support?

3. **Host Government Relations:** Social Ventures are often implemented in third-world or economically disadvantaged countries? Address any issues or actions required to gain host government support. Are there any potential resistance issues? Will the host government look upon your venture as a value-added initiative, or a threat? Are there additional fees, licenses, approvals, etc. that may impact implementation?

4. **Marketing:** Most potential investors and donors supporting a Social Entrepreneurship venture want to see a Marketing Plan. Who will you support? How will you reach them? How will you sell your idea? S-T-P is a standard marketing methodology that has stood the test of time. The concept is straight forward and depicted in Figure 11.4. Here is a quick breakout of the model.

Figure 10.4 S-T-P Model

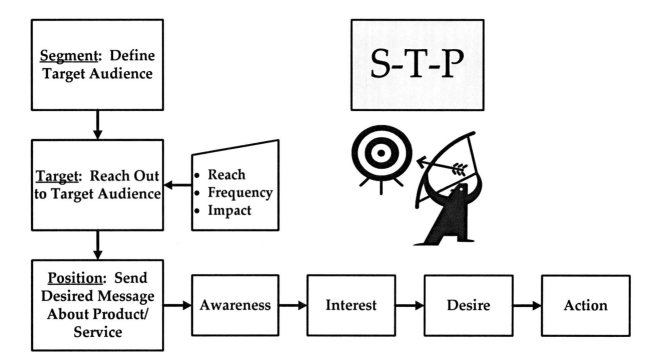

Figure 10.4 shares the S-T-P model and shows where "Reach, Frequency, Impact" (RFI) and "Awareness, Interest, Desire, Action" (AIDA) factors play a role in the overall Social Venture marketing mix.

- **Segment:** You must define the group(s) you plan to impact by your Social Venture. Segmentation can be defined by geographical area, gender, educational level, income level, age, etc. It is best to begin your venture by defining one or two key segments. Build your venture, and provide a solid proof of concept. Then expand to other segments. If you can show proof of concept, funds from investors, donors, and grants will be far more accessible.

- **Target:** How will you reach out to the segment you wish to impact? Will you use word of mouth, social media, radio, television, etc.? You also need to consider how often you need to target your selected segment(s) to ensure they get the message. There is a marketing acronym that is referred to as RFI. This acronym stands for "Reach, Frequency, and Impact" as noted above. You need to consider the level of difficulty you will encounter reaching your target segment, determine the frequency of your targeting efforts, and ensure the desired informational impact is achieved.

- **Position:** You need to position your message in a way to achieve buy-in and support. You want the segment(s) to adopt what you propose. Most targeted segments need to transition through a four-step adoption process before they are willing to accept a new product or service. This process can be defined by the acronym AIDA we introduced earlier. AIDA Is summarized as follows:

  1. **Awareness:** The first step in the product or service adoption process is to create awareness. This consists of positioning the "What" factors. "This is our product or service. The features are as follows..." Words are good for creating awareness. Visuals and hands-on activities are better.

  2. **Interest:** This step consists of providing the value proposition(s). This is also referred to as the "Why" or WII-FM factors. You need to catch the attention of your desired segment, and motivate them to listen and learn more about what you propose.

  3. **Desire:** Creating desire for your product or service is an important third step. At this point, the individual or group is able to associate the benefits of the proposed product or service to themselves. They want to be a part of your venture.

4. **Action:** The ultimate goal of introducing a new product or service is moving an individual or group into action. Actions consist of purchasing, using the product or service, buying-in, and/or participating. You must go through the first three steps to get to the point where action occurs.

The Social Entrepreneurship Business Case Summary

There are many similarities between the traditional Business Case, and those developed to launch a Social Entrepreneurship venture. The information provided in the first nine chapters of this book are very pertinent and worth reviewing. Remember the additional factors to consider we shared in this chapter.

- **Objectives:** You need to work diligently to define your objectives in terms of the social issue you plan to address. In addition, it is critical to define critical who, when, and where factors. Validate objectives by showing support from internal and external stakeholders and agencies.

- **Value Proposition:** There are additional stakeholders you must satisfy when launching a Social Entrepreneurship venture. Address the concerns of donors, grant providers, and other investors. The key issue to address again and again is your plan to sustain the venture once it gets started. Share this theme throughout the Business Case.

- **Cost and Benefits:** Take time to address specific sources for, and uses of, the financial support you receive. Ensure funds designated for a specific cost are applied as requested or directed. Develop a five-year plan to show how the organization will grow. Prove to donors, grant providers, and investors that you can sustain operations for the long-term. There's that word again—sustain! Yes, it is that important.

- **Risks:** There are both positive risks or opportunities, and negative risks or threats that could impact your Social Entrepreneurship venture. Address the top risks, and have responses ready for concerned stakeholders. If you don't have the right answers, funding may be jeopardized.

- **Other Supporting Information:** Do your homework. Find out what is on the minds of the many stakeholders whose support you need to be successful. Understand and address those issues. In addition, think S-T-P. How will you effectively market your venture to achieve your stated Mission and Vision?

We end this chapter with Figure 10.5. This is a quick and easy checklist you may want to use to determine the applicability of key areas discussed in this chapter.

Once you review the checklist and the "Food for Thought" sections, we will turn our attention to a different type of Business Case. This is a Business Case you develop, present, and approve to the most important person in your life—yourself! Chapter 11 will highlight "The Business Case for Life Decisions."

Figure 10.5 Social Entrepreneurship Checklist

Use this checklist to determine specific areas you need to address in your Business Case or overall Business Plan. For prioritization, we recommend the following indicators:

- **H: High**. A "Must Have."

- **M: Moderate**. A "Should Have."

- **L: Low**. A "Nice to Have."

- **N/A**: Not Applicable.

Component	Consideration	Priority	Comments
Objective	Accurate, Brief and Concise		
	Mission and Vision		
	Segmentation Definition		
	Time Phasing/Scheduling		
	Problem/Issue Support Data		
	Multi-Media Support		
Value Proposition (Financial)	Sustainment and Growth Summary		
	Funding/Grant Requirements		
	Unique Sales Position (USP)		
	"Triple Bottom Line" Goals		
	Scalability Options		
	Exit Strategy		
Value Proposition (Customer)	Adoption		
	Variations		
	Values		

Component	Consideration	Priority	Comments
Value Proposition (Internal Business or Process)	Environmental Improvement		
	Flexibility/Open to Ideas		
	Connections		
	Politics		
	Technology		
	Competition		
Value Proposition (Employee or Innovation and Learning)	Team Configuration		
	Cultural Liaison		
	Employee Motivation		
	Volunteer Motivation		
	Training		
Cost and Benefits	Cash Flow Diagram		
	Uses and Sources of Cash		
	Five Year Pro-Forma		
Risk	Legal/Regulatory		
	Financial		
	Project/Solution		
	Schedule		
	Cultural/Ethical		
	Resources		
Supporting Data and Information	Governance		
	Sustainment Plan		
	Host Government Relations		
	Marketing Plan		

Chapter 10 "Food For Thought"

Are you a Social Entrepreneur? Do you have a vision to make a difference through implementation of a great Social Venture? Use this template as a way to develop an initial game plan.

Business Case Component	Notes
Objective: What is my Social Venture?	
Value Proposition: What are my top 3 value propositions?	
Costs: What are initial costs?	
Benefits: What are the economic benefits that will help me sustain the venture?	

Business Case Component	Notes
Risks: What are risks that need to be addressed?	
Supporting Data and Information: What pertains?	

My Notes:

Chapter 11: The Business Case for Life Decisions

Traditional Business Cases are developed to present proposals to a decision-making body for approval. On the other hand, some Business Cases can be developed to determine a plan to enhance ourselves and our lives.

Figure 11.1 presents a Personal Balanced Scorecard model that has been adapted for the individual. This model shows four areas that an individual must balance to ensure health, happiness, and overall satisfaction.

Figure 11.1 Personal Balanced Scorecard

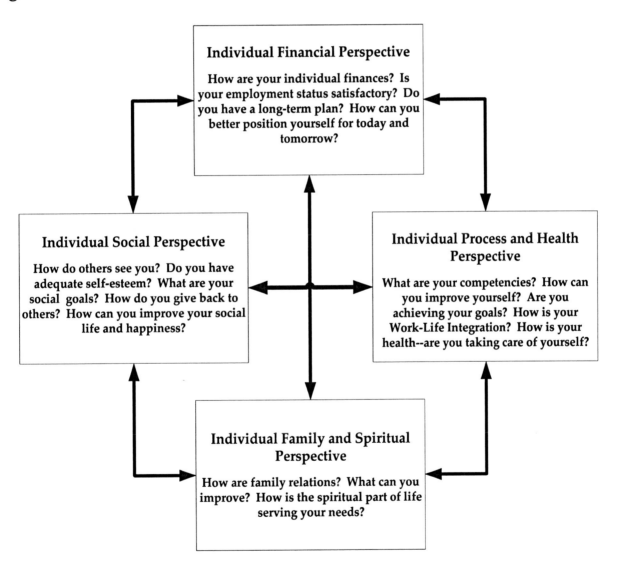

Individual Financial Perspective

How are your individual finances? Is your employment status satisfactory? Do you have a long-term plan? How can you better position yourself for today and tomorrow?

Individual Social Perspective

How do others see you? Do you have adequate self-esteem? What are your social goals? How do you give back to others? How can you improve your social life and happiness?

Individual Process and Health Perspective

What are your competencies? How can you improve yourself? Are you achieving your goals? How is your Work-Life Integration? How is your health--are you taking care of yourself?

Individual Family and Spiritual Perspective

How are family relations? What can you improve? How is the spiritual part of life serving your needs?

Individual Financial Perspective

Financial stability is a necessary Critical Success Factor for everyone today. Whether we like it or not, we must be able to support ourselves, and those who depend upon us. The individual financial perspective asks key questions that impact your everyday life.

- **How are your individual finances?** Are you making adequate salary? Do you have enough money left over to pay the bills and still put something away for the future? Leading financial planners tell us we should have the equivalent of at least six-month's salary in savings. They also state that a best practice is to save and invest 5 to 10% each pay period for the future.

- **Is your employment status satisfactory?** The job market is a moving target. New employment opportunities come and go. Are you in a secure position? If so, how can you maintain your secure status? If not, what is your exit strategy? You may need to move to the next job opportunity that suits your passion and talents. Change is continual. Be ready when it comes.

- **Do you have a long-term plan?** How much will you need for retirement to live comfortably? How well are you proceeding to achieve your future financial goals? Ray Lucia[12] lays out three goals in his book "Buckets of Money". The book is a great read! Have a plan for today, for the near-term, and the long-term.

- **Do you have a Plan B?** How will you support your family if you become disabled, or are no longer able to provide adequate income for a variety of reasons? Do you have adequate Life and Health Insurance?

- **How can you better position yourself for today and tomorrow?** What is your financial self-vision for the future? Where do you see yourself in 5 years, 10 years? Do you have a plan to get to where you want to be?

---

[12] *Buckets of Money*, Ray Lucia

Individual Process and Health Perspective

The competencies and skills you possess will help you to achieve both personal and individual financial goals. In addition, your health is a consideration that drives everything you do. Here are some additional considerations you need to consider to balance your Personal Balanced Scorecard.

- **What are your competencies?** Do you possess the skills you both need and want to be successful and happy? Some skills may be necessary to help you achieve financial goals. Others may be necessary to help you achieve individual goals such as pursuit of hobbies. Enjoying life is important.

- **How can you improve yourself?** Take a look at who you are versus who you want to become. Map out a plan to get to where you want to be.

- **Are you achieving your goals?** If you have goals and a plan, how is it working? Are you on-track, or do you need to get back on-track?

- **How is your Work Life Integration?** A healthy lifestyle is best served when you develop a balance between work and other activities that suit you. For some people, that may be 70% work and 30% non-work activities. For others, the percentages may be reversed. Where are you? Do you need to adjust your percentages?

- **How is your health--are you taking care of yourself?** This is a critical question. Health is our number one asset. Without health, nothing else eventually matters. Are you taking care of yourself? Are you eating right and exercising regularly? How can you improve and stay fit? Ensure this is part of your personal Business Case!

Individual Family and Spiritual Perspective

This part of the Personal Balanced Scorecard is important as well. Everyone has family. There are parents, sisters and brothers, relatives, spouses, significant others, children, etc. who play important roles in determining who we are. There is an old saying. "One day your work days may come to an end. However, family is forever." The spiritual part of some people's lives can also make a huge positive difference. This third perspective must be addressed and balanced as well.

- **How are family relations?** Your relationship with your family can translate to high-levels of happiness or sadness. Evaluate your relationships with family members. Ask yourself if you are happy with the current state of your relationships. If so, add a few activities to sustain the positives you've achieved. If not, think of some ways to improve.

- **What can you improve?** It is impossible for a human being to be everything to everyone. However, there may be some ways you can change or grow that will add to family member's happiness. For example, if you have a daughter (as I do) who is inspired by music, take an interest in her hopes and dreams. Learn a bit about her passions. Talk with her about the subject. You will achieve a high-level of reward for your efforts. My daughter Erika is a prime example. Take my advice, sharing and caring works.

- **How is the spiritual part of life serving your needs?** There are many people who place religion high in importance in their lives? If this is you, evaluate your relationship with your church of choice. Are you happy with the current relationship? If so, sustain. If you do not feel you are where you need to be spiritually, add a line item to your personal Business Case and strive to be where you want to be.

Individual Social Perspective

The individual social perspective of the Personal Balanced Scorecard is the final section. This part of the scorecard deals with your social environment. People often state, "No man is an island." We depend on relationships with others in the business and personal environment. This key area must be considered in every individual Business Case, and balanced with the other three perspectives.

- **How do others see you?** I've sometimes heard people say, "I don't care what other people think." In most cases, however, the statement is at best only partially true. Most people "do care" to some extent. Try to map out characteristics and attributes you want others to see in you. Then, make a plan to refine your image to reflect the characteristics and attributes you want to portray.

- **Do you have adequate self-esteem?** There is a reality in life. If we are not happy with ourselves, it is difficult to be happy about most other aspects in life. When you look in the mirror, who do you see? Do you see someone you are proud of? Or do you see someone you would like to change? If the answer is the latter, make those changes. You have unique gifts and talents that make you special! Tap into those talents and become the person you truly want to be. Believe it or not, it *is* within your reach.

- **How do you give back to others?** There are many in this world less fortunate than you? How can I make that statement? You are reading this book. You obviously are motivated to improve your competencies and abilities. You are obviously literate, motivated, and driven to action. Share your passion and gifts with others. Inspire and help them! Make a difference in another's life.

- **How can you improve your social life and happiness?** Be like Santa Claus. Make a list and check it twice. ☺ Look at where you are from a social and happiness standpoint, where you really want to be, and take a few positive actions to get there! Value friendships. It pays!

Developing Your Personal Business Case

We discussed the SWOT concept in Chapter 7. This concept is a great way to determine the best approach to incrementally improve your personal standing in all four individual Personal Balanced Scorecard perspectives. Figure 11.2 shows an adaptation of a SWOT scorecard you can easily adapt to your situation. Use it, enjoy, and climb the mountain of happiness and success.

Figure 11.2 Individual Quantified SWOT Analysis

Personal Business Case for John Doe for 1 April to 30 June, 20xx					
Goal	Category	Importance	Impact	Score	Plan
1. Improve fitness	Process & Health	5	5	25	Gym weekly x 3
2. Position self for better job	Financial	4	5	20	Update and post new resume
3. Create family day	Family & Spiritual	5	4	20	2x monthly
4. Improve appearance	Social	3	3	9	New clothing purchase trip
5. Attain a Quality Certification	Process & Health	3	5	15	Certified Quality Manager
6. Double my savings	Financial	3	4	12	Payroll deduction preferred
7. Attend church regularly	Family & Spiritual	3	3	9	At least 3x monthly
8. Increase donations to charity	Social	2	3	6	Cancer/Heart charities monthly

Here are some key points to remember when developing your individual Business Case using the SWOT hybrid approach.

- Your analysis should be developed for a short period of time. A flexible three-month plan is optimal.

- Use a standard scoring system. In this example, we score importance and impact on a one-to-five basis. A score of five is high and one is low.

- Choose a goal to accomplish in each of the four Personal Balanced Scorecard areas. All areas must be in balance. In this example, "Improve Appearance" is your #4 priority despite the fact it scores less than some other goals. Pick the top scoring priority in each of the four individual Personal Balanced Scorecard perspectives.

- Try to satisfy all goals. However, work on the top four goals first. At the end of the three-month period, evaluate where you are. If you achieved a goal, take it off the list. Move the second ranked goal in that category up and define a new goal in the same category to replace the goal that you just completed.

- A total of eight goals are optimal. Pick two in each category. Don't set yourself up for failure by trying to do too much too quickly. It is better to achieve one or two goals than to begin working on all eight, and complete zero.

The Business Case for Life Decisions Summary

Keep an eye on the most important asset you possess—yourself. Develop a Business Case for improvement in the four individual Personal Balanced Scorecard perspectives shared in Figure 11.1, and sell yourself on the importance to approve and implement the plan. You will be rewarded with an improved quality of life in return for your investment! You will notice the benefits, and so will others around you.

Chapter 11 "Food For Thought"

Think about a potential Business Case to improve you. Which areas of the Personal Balanced Scorecard do you want to improve?

The Business Case for Life Decisions	
Financial Perspective	Process and Health Perspective
Social Perspective	Family and Spiritual Perspective

My Notes:

Turn Great Ideas into Reality: Develop and Present a Winning Business Case Final Thoughts

Thank you for purchasing this book. We hope you found the information contained to be pertinent and useful. The two keys to developing a winning Business Case are preparation and presentation.

The first seven chapters of this book described the basic components and considerations of a winning Business Case. Our goal was to provide as many potential considerations as we could think of to help you prepare. There may be some areas that do not pertain to your Business Case. If so, there is no need to address those areas. There may be other areas we did not address that are pertinent due to the uniqueness of your company or organization. Please include those areas as applicable.

Chapters 8 and 9 describe the presentation piece of the puzzle. How you present is critically important, and can often determine success or failure. We urge you to adopt and use the standard templates we shared. They are proven winners used by effective presenters. In addition, we highly encourage you to use the five-step presentation methodology summarized in Chapter 9. This works superbly as well!

Chapters 10 and 11 addressed specific Business Case types for the Social Entrepreneur and introduced the "Business Case for Life Decisions." We hope this additional information adds value to our overall book.

We always appreciate feedback. Feel free to address the author at dan@becauz.com or daniel.yeomans@roisc.com. We will also send a free PowerPoint file in PDF form that tracks to the first nine chapters in this book simply for asking! This is included in the price of the book! ☺

We also provide virtual seminars, on-premise seminars, or a cadre of professionals to support your specific individual or corporate needs at very reasonable costs. Contact us if we can be of assistance! Thank you again—we hope that all your Business Cases are a resounding success!

Appendix A: Acronym List

Acronym	Long Title
5W+H	What, Why, Who, When, Where + How
ABC	Accurate, Brief, Concise
AIDA	Awareness, Interest, Desire, Action
BC/DR	Business Continuance/Disaster Recovery
BHAG	Big Hairy Audacious Goal
CAPEX	Capital Expenses
CEO	Chief Executive Officer
CMQ/OE ®	Certified Manager of Quality/Organizational Excellence
COGS	Cost of Goods Sold
CPE	Customer Partnership Experience
CSAT	Customer Satisfaction
CSF	Critical Success Factor
CSR	Corporate Social Responsibility
DMAIC	Define, Measure, Analyze, Improve, Control
EPS	Earnings per Share
FAQ	Frequently Asked Questions
FURPS	Functionality, Usability, Reliability, Performance, Supportability
IRR	Internal Rate of Return
ISO	International Organization for Standardization
KISS	Keep it Short and Sweet
NPV	Net Present Value
NSAT	Net Satisfaction
OPEX	Operational Expenses
OSHA	Occupational Safety and Health Administration
OTP	Opportunity, Target, Proposal

Acronym	Long Title
PDCA	Plan, Do, Check, Act
PERT	Program Evaluation and Review Technique
PIE	Persuade, Inform, Entertain
PIP	Persuade, Inform, Persuade
PMBOK®Guide	Project Management Body of Knowledge
PMI ®	Project Management Institute ®
PMP ®	Project Management Professional ®
PNP	Positive, Negative, Positive
PROI	Productivity Return on Investment
PSB	Problem, Solution, Benefit
QC	Quality Control
RACI	Responsible, Accountable, Consult, Inform
RBS	Risk Breakdown Structure
RFI	Reach, Frequency, Impact
RMP ®	Risk Management Professional ®
ROI	Return on Investment
ROM	Rough Order of Magnitude
SD	Standard Deviation
SLA	Service Level Agreement
SMARTWAY	Specific, Measurable, Attainable, Relevant, Target Driven, Worth Implementing, Assignable, Yields Results
SME	Subject Matter Expert
SOX	Sarbanes-Oxley
STP	Situation, Target, Proposal
S-T-P	Segment, Target, Position
SWOT	Strengths, Weaknesses, Opportunities, Threats
TCO	Total Cost of Ownership

Acronym	Long Title
TQM	Total Quality Management
USP	Unique Selling Position
WBS	Work Breakdown Structure
WII-FM	"What's in it for me?"

Appendix B: Glossary of Terms

Term	Definition
5W+H Presentation Method	The 5W+H presentation method works well when you have key information you want to provide in some priority order. The 5W+H stands for What, Why, Who, When, Where, and How.
Acceptance (Accept)	This response entails taking no immediate action until the risk occurs. There are two types of acceptance strategies. One is passive (no risk response developed) and the other is active (risk response developed).
Adoption	The process of attaining employee and customer buy-in to support a proposal for a new product or service. Effective change management aids in attaining adoption.
Affinity Charting/Mind Mapping	Method uses the intellectual power of a group to place risks into categories. This is the best method to use if you believe you have not identified all possible risks. Mind Mapping is application of the same process by a single individual.
AIDA	Most targeted segments need to transition through a four-step adoption process before they are willing to accept a new product or service. This process can be defined by the acronym AIDA. It stands for Awareness, Interest, Desire, and Action.
Analytical Thinking	A thinking attribute of Emergenetics. Characterized by clear thinking, logical problem solving, math enjoyment, rational thinking, and learning by mental analysis.
Architecture	Architecture is an organized set of consensus decisions on policies and principles, services and common solutions, standards and guidelines, as well as specific vendor products used by an organization.
Apply the Grease	Coordinate a presentation ahead of time with key stakeholders to gain support. Conduct the "meeting before the meeting" to work issues before a formal presentation.

Term	Definition
Assignable	Component of SMARTWAY. Shows availability of necessary capacity and skill sets required to deliver a Business Case proposal. Shows proposal is important enough to warrant trade-offs from other projects?
Assumption	Information we believe to be true but have not yet validated. Assumptions are always risks until validated.
Assumptions Analysis	Action of validating or dismissing an assumption through analysis and research.
Attainable	Component of SMARTWAY. Ensures a project can be accomplished in the current environment. Considerations include economic circumstances, legal and compliance, technology, culture, social considerations, internal and external politics, and physical/logistical factors.
Attention Step	Part of a five-step approach to effective presenting. Provides an overview of "What" the Business Case proposes in a compelling manner.
Automation	Proposal to automate a manual process. Goal is to improve time and reduce resources. Generally improves efficiency.
Avoidance (Avoid)	The focus of this risk response strategy is to eliminate the cause of a negative risk. Try to take action to ensure the risk does not occur. This is often accomplished by removing people and/or activities.
Balanced Scorecard	Robert S. Kaplan and David P. Norton created the Balanced Scorecard. The model defines objectives a business needs to satisfy to sustain and grow. The Balanced Scorecard can be used in a Business Case to show reasons "Why" a project should be undertaken.
Bookable	Any cost or revenue adjustment that can impact the actual budget. A bookable cost must be added to the budget. A bookable benefit is a cost that can actually be reduced from the budget. It is real cost savings you can "take to the bank."

Term	Definition
Brainstorming	Open forum where members generate ideas and solve problems. A facilitator logs inputs. Brainstorming is one method used to attain expert input.
Business Case	Describes the reasoning to initiate or kill a proposed project or activity. Most Business Cases are normally developed and presented in the form of a well-structured written proposal.
Capital Expenses (CAPEX)	CAPEX funds are used to purchase buildings, equipment, or other assets with a long life. In most cases, assets purchased with CAPEX funds are subject to depreciation.
Cash Flow Diagram	A diagram that shows time-phased investments (Costs) and revenues (Benefits) derived from a project. Generally used to calculate key financial metrics.
Cause and Effect Diagrams	Graphic depictions of risk causes and potential effects impacting a project or proposal. Also called Ishikawa Diagram, Root Cause Identification, or Fishbone Diagram.
Communications Blockers	Any distractions or noise factors that can interrupt or inhibit successful communications. For example, physical noise, culture, acronyms and jargon, etc.
Competitive Advantage	Improve the ability possessed by an organization to produce high-quality products or services as compared to other external competitors.
Complaints Management	Address customer complaints and propose solutions to reduce or eliminate issues. Requests may be generated from internal or external sources.
Compliance/Legal	Ensure key compliance or legal requirements are met. Reduce risks of non-compliance. May include regulatory considerations.
Conceptual Thinking	A thinking attribute of Emergenetics. Characterized by imaginative thinking, intuitive about ideas, visionary, enjoys the unusual, and learns by experimenting.
Conclusion & Next Steps	Part of a five-step approach to effective presenting. The segment of the presentation where you present your recommendation and solicit feedback.

Term	Definition
Constraints	Anything that can limit the team's options. Boundaries that must be acknowledged and addressed. Typical constraints include time, cost, scope, quality, resources, customer satisfaction, and risk.
Contingency Funds	Reserves set aside to accommodate risk events. These are generally Contingency Reserves for known risks, or Management Reserves for unknown risks.
Contingency Plan	Your primary response plan to address a risk. The secondary plan is referred to as a "Fallback Plan."
Contingency Reserves	Extra time or budget added to a project to account for known risks. Also referred to as reserves for "known unknowns."
Contingency Response Strategy	A risk response strategy that identifies triggers. Triggers allow for initiation of a response strategy before the actual risk event occurs.
Core Competencies	Competencies essential for your organization to maintain a competitive advantage.
Cost Avoidance	Eliminate the need to spend funds allocated in the budget. Eliminate funds expenditures for prior approved projects.
Cost Savings	Reduce the real costs of doing business. These savings are "bookable." They reduce your budget.
Creativity	Creative employees think of new ways to do business and add value. Employee surveys note the ability to be creative as a key reason they stay with a company.
Critical Success Factors (CSF)	Critical Success Factors drive every organization. A solid Business Case identifies CSF, and addresses how the organization is performing them. A Business Case should propose ways to improve CSF performance.

Term	Definition
Customer Satisfaction (CSAT)	CSAT is a key measure of customer satisfaction. Goal is to increase scores.
Customer Partnership Experience (CPE)	Customer level of satisfaction regarding areas of customer service and product/service value.
Customer Perspective	Component of the Balanced Scorecard. Considers: How do our customers see us? What are our customer-based goals? How can we better serve our customer base?
Decision Tree Analysis	Describes a scenario under consideration and uses available data to determine the most economic approach. The primary objective is to determine which scenarios provide the best overall Expected Monetary Value (EMV).
Definitive Statement	Method of capturing an audience's attention. Provide a compelling statement of fact that you know is of interest to the audience.
Delphi Technique	Gain inputs and consensus through inputs kept anonymous. Reduces fear of reprisal. Delphi Technique is also a method used to attain expert input. Surveys and questionnaires are popular data collection methods.
Dependencies	Any constraint that dictates orderly accomplishment of project activities. External dependencies are regulatory. Discretionary dependencies reduce risk. Mandatory dependencies cannot be broken.
Depreciation	Equipment and assets lose value as you use them. In business, you are able to claim lost value of assets you purchase. The value lost on an annual basis is claimed as depreciation.
Development/ Construction Costs	Costs associated with developing or building the product or service proposed in a Business Case. May be OPEX or CAPEX costs.
Devil's Advocate Approach	Ask team members and colleagues to review your Business Case and think of any reasons not to approve the proposal. Build around these objections, anticipate questions, and plan responses ahead of time.

Term	Definition
Direct Costs	Direct costs are funds you must pay out. Subcategories of these costs are fixed costs you must pay for set-up or lease fees, and variable costs which are based on production.
Discount Rate	The percentage value used to calculate the impact of time on cash flow. Used when calculating Net Present Value. Also referred to as "Cost of Capital."
DMAIC	A five-step methodology for process improvement. Define the process, Measure the process, Analyze performance, Improve the process, and Control results.
Earnings per Share (EPS)	Increase overall corporate Earnings per Share from common stock. Places corporation into a positive light in investor's minds.
Effectiveness	Improve corporate product or service delivery to the satisfaction of your customer base (Ties into the Customer Perspective of the Balanced Scorecard). Customers define effectiveness.
Efficiency	Present ideas that allow the organization to work more economically. Measure of time and resources required to implement a process.
Emergenetics ®	A brain-based approach to personality profiling that gives you the keys to discover not only your own natural strengths and talents, but also those of others.
Employee or Innovation and Learning Perspective	Component of the Balanced Scorecard. Considers: Can we continue to improve and create value? Is our employee force equipped/trained to succeed? How can we improve morale and employee passion?
Enhancement (Enhance)	This risk response aims to increase the probability of a risk occurring or the impact of a risk if it occurs. This response supports positive risks.
Executive Summary	A high-level overview of a Business Case that defines objectives, the value proposition, and general information at a high-level. Normally the first overview of a Business Casethat decision makers see.

Term	Definition
Expected Monetary Value (EMV)	Method used to establish Contingency Reserve requirements for both budget and schedules. EMV is quantified by multiplying probability times the best or worst case cost/time scenario.
Exploitation (Exploit)	This is a risk response where you take action to make a cause occur. You work to make the risk happen. It may require additional time or resources to use the exploit response method. This response supports positive risks.
External Support Costs	Costs to procure external resources needed to achieve objectives of a Business Case. May address parts, supplies, materials, marketing, advertising, etc.
Filler Words	Filler words are those verbal pauses and missteps like "Um and Ah", or thrown in words such as "Ya Know or Like."
Financial Perspective	Component of the Balanced Scorecard. Considers: How do we look to our shareholders? How can we improve our financial position? How can we become more effective?
Fishbone Diagram	See *Cause and Effect Diagrams*
Fixed Costs	Any cost incurred prior to production. Generally initial set-up costs, lease costs, equipment purchases, etc.
Functionality	Component of the FURPS Model. Customers want products and services that provide the functionality they need to be successful. They expect products that are flexible, scalable, and sustainable.
FURPS Model	The FURPS model is used by many product and service developers to explain the five critical concerns of customers when it comes to purchasing decisions.
Group Creativity Techniques	Tools and techniques designed to tap into the group's creative minds and extract the information you need. Includes Brainstorming, Nominal Group Technique, Delphi Technique, and Mind Mapping/Affinity Charting.

Term	Definition
Governance	Corporate Governance can be defined as policies and processes to oversee the direction and management of the firm to ensure it fulfills its mandate.
Hard Benefits	Hard benefits are also referred to as bookable benefits. These benefits provide additional working capital by increasing cash assets or reducing cash liabilities.
Hardware Costs	Any hardware, software, or fixed equipment assets required to implement a proposed project. This is normally a CAPEX cost.
Histogram	A bar chart that shows how variables occur over time. For example, a Histogram could show the number of complaints that occurred over a three-month period.
Improve Quality	Present ideas that reduce waste, eliminate workarounds, lower amounts of warranty work, etc.
Increase Revenue	Increase revenue through additional sales, market share, etc. Take advantage of market opportunities.
Indirect Costs	Indirect costs are costs that will be incurred by your project. However, these costs do not need to be accounted for in your project budget. Example: Utilities.
Individual Family and Spiritual Perspective	Personal Balanced Scorecard Component. Poses the questions: How are family relations? What can you improve? How is the spiritual part of life serving your needs?
Individual Financial Perspective	Personal Balanced Scorecard Component. Poses the questions: How are your individual finances? Is your employment status satisfactory? Do you have a long-term plan? How can you better position yourself for today and tomorrow?
Individual Process and Health Perspective	Personal Balanced Scorecard Component. Poses the questions: What are your competencies? How can you improve yourself? Are you achieving your goals? How is your Work Life Integration? How is your health--are you taking care of yourself?

Term	Definition
Individual Social Perspective	Personal Balanced Scorecard Component. Poses the questions: How do others see you? Do you have adequate self-esteem? What are your social goals? How do you give back to others? How can you improve your social life and happiness?
Influence Diagrams	Method includes graphical representations of situations showing causal influences, time ordering of events, and other relationships between variables and outcomes.
Information Gathering Techniques	Methods for gathering information. Includes Brainstorming, Delphi Technique, Interviews, Root Cause Identification, and Nominal Group Technique.
Internal Business or Process Perspective	Component of the Balanced Scorecard. Considers: What core competencies must we excel at? How can we improve processes? How can we become more efficient?
Internal Rate of Return (IRR)	Financial metric that provides a percentage evaluation of a project's cash flow. IRR looks at the Net Present Value of costs and compares it to the Net Present Value of benefits as they are paid out (costs) or accrued (benefits) over time.
Internal Support Costs	Costs incurred to pay for the project team and other internal Subject Matter Experts. Costs are indirect if they are not part of the project budget. They are direct costs if part of the project budget.
Interview	One-on-one meetings with key stakeholders or experts in a given field. A drawback of this technique is that it takes time and is slow.
Ishikawa Diagram	See *Cause and Effect Diagrams*
Known Risks	Positive or negative risks identified that may impact a Business Case or project. Known risks are generally recorded on a Risk Register.
Leverage Employee Skills	Projects that allow employees to leverage their skills to a greater extent add value and improve morale. Use the talents of your employees.

Term	Definition
Lewin Change Model	The Lewin Change Model provides a three-step process that has proven successful in managing change. Steps include unfreeze, transition, and refreeze.
Licenses/Permit Costs	Any costs associated with licensing or permit requirements. Could include legal or compliance related fees as well.
Management Reserves	Extra time or budget added to a project to account for unknown risks. Also referred to as reserves for unknown unknowns.
Materials/Supply Costs	Costs incurred for any consumable materials or supplies needed to implement a proposed project. May include books, tools, etc. These are OPEX costs that may be incurred prior to project initiation, and as the project is being planned and executed.
Measureable	Component of SMARTWAY. Ensure project objectives are measurable. Be able to draw a picture of what a successful project outcome looks like. If possible, use a measure that reflects the current state (As Is), and contrast it to a target (To Be) state that has meaning to the audience.
Mitigation (Mitigate)	Risk response that takes actions to reduce the probability of a negative risk occurring, or the impact of risk if it occurs. This could be thought of as developing a Plan B.
Morale and Passion	Some projects have potential to improve employee morale and passion for the job. These are valuable initiatives that increase motivation.
Motivation Step	Part of a five-step approach to effective presenting. Provides an overview of "Why" the Business Case adds value in a compelling manner.
Negative Risk	Any risk event that may result in a threat to project objectives. Applicable responses include avoid, transfer, mitigate, or accept.
Net PresentValue (NPV)	Financial metric that provides positive or negative cash value to evaluate the merit of a project. NPV applies a discount rate to all costs and benefits to determine the real cash value of a project based on the value of money today.

Term	Definition
Nominal Group Technique	Technique similar to Brainstorming. Collect input from a select group. Analyze inputs, and then rank order the results.
Non-Verbal Communications	Communications that are relayed through our facial expressions, gestures, intonation, etc. Non-verbal communications comprise approximately 55% of the total message according to the Project Management Institute.
Normal Distribution	Normal distribution is also referred to as the "Bell Curve." A normal distribution model uses averages and "Sigma" intervals to show the potential range of values over the length of a bell curve.
Net Satisfaction (NSAT)	NSAT is a key measure of customer satisfaction. The goal is to increase the overall NSAT score. Higher is better.
Objectives	State "What" you propose. The statement must be accurate, brief, and concise. Solid objectives consist of two parts—an action and a result.
One-Point Estimating	A cost and benefit estimating method that only considers the most likely estimate. One-Point Estimating is generally accurate only 10 – 15% of the time.
Operational Expenses (OPEX)	OPEX funds are generally used to accommodate the ongoing costs for running a product, business, or system. In general, we can say OPEX funds are used to sustain the business. They are generally included in the annual operating budget.
Pareto Chart	A bar chart that shows variables as issues, problems, events, etc. in order of their frequency of occurrence; left to right. The Pareto Principle contends that 20% of the causes lead to 80% of the effects. The idea is to address the variable that occurs most frequently.
Parking Lot	A meeting management technique where you mutually agree to discuss an issue at a later time so as not to detract from achieving meeting objectives. Table a conversation until later.

Term	Definition
Payback	Financial metric that does not consider the total life of a project. It is a metric that calculates how long it will take to recover the initial investment cost, and can be measured in years, months, or days.
Performance	Component of the FURPS Model. The ability of a product or service to deliver functionality in a timely manner that meets customer needs.
Personal Balanced Scorecard	A Balanced Scorecard model that has been adapted for the individual. This model shows four areas impacting an individual that must be balanced to ensure health, happiness, and personal satisfaction.
PERT	Program Evaluation and Review Technique. A form of Three-Point Estimating that uses a weighted method to calculate the best estimate based on pessimistic, most likely, and optimistic cost and/or benefit inputs.
PIE	Acronym that stands for the three potential objectives of a presentation. These include persuade, inform, and/or entertain.
PIP Presentation Method	The PIP presentation method works well when you believe you have an urgent value proposition that needs to be fulfilled. The acronym stands for "Persuade, Inform, and Persuade."
PNP Presentation Method	The PNP presentation method is best suited when you are performing well in an area, but believe you have an opportunity to improve. The PNP acronym stands for "Positive, Negative, Positive."
Portfolio/Program Support	Implement projects that will allow a business to accomplish its Mission, Vision and high-level goals to move the company forward. Address and close gaps.
Position	A step in the marketing S-T-P process. You need to position your message in a way to achieve buy-in and support. You want the segment to adopt what you propose.
Positive Risk	Any risk event that may result in an opportunity to improve or enhance project objectives. Applicable responses include exploit, share, enhance, or accept.

Term	Definition
Pre-Mortem	Method used to identify potential risks prior to project planning and execution. Compare your project to past projects that were similar. Try to determine what could go right or wrong with your project before the project begins.
Presentation Body	Part of a five-step approach to effective presenting. The body of the presentation. Best accomplished by using a standard template model (STP, OTP, PSB, etc.).
Process Improvement	Present ideas that will allow your organization to improve overall process performance. In addition, determine if your Business Case will positively impact dependent processes to better work together.
Process Mapping	Define and document key processes critical to the success of your organization. Improve knowledge and understanding of core processes.
Productivity Return on Investment (PROI)	A benefit of improving process efficiency. Calculate by multiplying the number of hours saved times the average employee salary. For example, we saved 50 hours for employees making $20 per hour. PROI is $1,000.
Pro-Forma Income Statement	Many investors want to see a five-year plan before investing. Their objective is to ensure your venture is sustainable over the long-term. In addition, they want to see where they potentially will fit into the plan. The Pro-Forma Income Statement shares this information.
PSB Presentation Method	PSB is an acronym that stands for "Problem, Solution, and Benefits (PSB)." It works well when there is a recognized problem, and you want to stress your solution to solve the problem, and share the associated benefits.
Qualitative Risk Analysis	Subjective risk evaluation process where risks are scored and prioritized using the formula probability times the impact.
RACI	Common method used to show roles and responsibilities. Assigns stakeholders as Responsible, Accountable, Consult, or Inform.

Term	Definition
Reach, Frequency, and Impact (RFI)	A measure of the reach and frequency requirements for a marketing message to achieve the desired impact from a targeted segment.
Redirecting	Precision questioning technique. Redirect a question that is beyond your scope of understanding to a Subject Matter Expert (SME). Anticipate questions you may receive, and have the right people available to provide a response on your behalf.
Reduce Process Resource Requirements	Reduce number of resources required to implement core processes. Enhance overall productivity. This is a key goal of efficiency.
Reduce Process Time	Achieve "Lean" goals or opportunities by reducing time to perform key processes. This is a key goal of efficiency.
Relevant	Component of SMARTWAY. Show how your project fits in the overall corporate or organizational big picture. Strive for traceability.
Reliability	Component of the FURPS Model. The ability of a product or service to deliver functionality without failure or excessive downtime.
Remotivation Step	Part of a five-step approach to effective presenting. The final thrust of a presentation. Reiterates a key value proposition offered by a Business Case proposal.
Rephrasing	Precision questioning technique. Rephrase a question to allow for an easier response. In some cases, a decision maker may pose a long, drawn out question that has many sub points. Try to rephrase the question in a simpler form and respond accordingly.
Reserve Analysis	Process of reviewing Management Reserves and Contingency Reserves to ensure they support project needs. These are reserves to address risk events.
Reserves	Extra time or budget added to a project to account for risks. Effective risk management provides a basis for identifying and requesting reserves.

Term	Definition
Residual Risks	Potential risk impacts that remain after a risk response is executed. For example, a risk response may address 80% of the impacts of a risk event. The Residual Risk is the 20% that remains.
Return on Investment (ROI)	Financial metric that provides a percentage evaluation of a project's cash flow. Compares costs and benefits. Does not consider the Present Value of Money.
Reversing	Precision questioning technique. Reversing a question is removing a negative cast from the question, and turning it positive through your response.
Rhetorical Question	Method of capturing an audience's attention. Pose a question to the group with an obvious answer. The answer to the question, however, should resonate with the audience. Pause to allow the intent of the question to "sink in."
Risk	An uncertain event or condition that, if it occurs, has a positive or negative effect on at least one of the project's objectives.
Risk Averse	Indicates stakeholder unwillingness to accept certain categories or types of risk. For example, some stakeholders may have an adversity to cost risks.
Risk Breakdown Structure (RBS)	Lists risk categories and sub-categories in hierarchical order to help identify risks. Places risks in categories, and defines specific risks applicable to the type of project being managed in that category.
Risk Management (Opportunities)	Take action to make positive risk events occur that will lead to opportunities. Enhance probability and impact of such events.
Risk Management (Threats)	Reduce the causes, probability, or impact of potential negative risks, or threats, that could impact a project.
Risk Rating	A score that reflects the probability or impact of an individual risk event.

Term	Definition
Risk Register	Tool used to record, document, prioritize, and manage risks. Lists both positive and negative risks.
Risk Score	A score that reflects the uncertainty of an individual risk by multiplying the Probability Risk Rating times the Impact Risk Rating.
Risk Tolerance	A statement of how much risk a stakeholder is willing to tolerate. Generally stems from risk attitudes.
Risk Utility	Describes a person or organization's willingness to accept risk. *See Risk Averse*
Root Cause Identification	See *Cause and Effect Diagrams*
Rough Order of Magnitude (ROM)	A Rough Order of Magnitude (ROM) level estimate is +/- 50% of what you estimate will be the actual costs of the project you are proposing.
Rule of 3 (Options)	Common practice to include at least three options or recommendations in a Business Case. Generally includes an "As Is" or "Do Nothing" option.
Run Chart	Chart that shows how a variable changes over time. Variable quantities are reflected in form of a line. For example, a Run Chart could provide a linear view of sales over a one-year period.
Satisfy Shareholders	Implement projects key shareholders deem as having value. Respond to shareholder needs and requests.
Secondary Risk	Any new risk resulting from a planned risk response. Secondary risks should not have a higher Risk Score than the primary risk you developed the initial risk response for.

Term	Definition
Segment	A step in the marketing S-T-P process. You must define the group you plan to impact by your Social Entrepreneurship venture. Segmentation can be defined by geographical area, gender, educational level, income level, age, etc.
Service Level Agreement (SLA)	A measure of performance that an organization strives to satisfy in support of partners, customers, etc. For example, we promise 95% system reliability.
Sharing (Share)	This risk response enlists the support of a third-party to take advantage of the opportunities presented by a positive risk event. You partner with a third-party, and both share in the benefits.
SMARTWAY	A model that describes the attributes a solid Business Case objective should satisfy. See the Glossary for a list of specific components.
Smoothing	Conflict management technique that attempts to find a foundational point of agreement for all stakeholders that can be built upon.
Social Entrepreneur	A Social Entrepreneur recognizes a social problem and uses sound business practices to organize, create and manage a venture to achieve social change. This goal is referred to as a Social Venture.
Social Thinking	A thinking attribute of Emergenetics. Characterized by intuitive about people, social awareness, sympathetic, empathetic, and learns from others.
Social Venture	A Business Case proposal from a Social Entrepreneur to positively address an issue impacting society, and alleviate the problem.
Soft Benefits	Benefits that do not directly translate into increased cash flow or potential to reduce bookable operating costs in an organization's budget. Benefits may include increased morale, productivity, time savings, customer satisfaction, reduced risk, etc.
Specific	Component of SMARTWAY. State a specific action and result in simple terms that are understood by the audience segment you are addressing. Ambiguity is the enemy.

Term	Definition
Stakeholder	Any individual or organization with an interest in the project. Stakeholders are both internal and external.
Stakeholder Register	List that includes key information about stakeholders. Normally includes: Identification information, Assessment Information, and Stakeholder Classification.
STP/OTP Presentation Method	STP or OTP is the acronym for the "Situation, Target, Proposal (STP)" or "Opportunity, Target, Proposal (OTP)" presentation template. These methods are highly effective when you have quantitative data or metrics to substantiate a proposal.
Structural Thinking	A thinking attribute of Emergenetics. Characterized by practical thinking, appreciation of guidelines, cautious on new ideas, predictable, and learns by doing.
Subject Matter Expert (SME)	Individual or group that provides technical information and support you need for successful accomplishment of a Business Case or project. Oftentimes an internal or external consultant.
Support Costs	Any costs incurred at completion of the project. These are normally OPEX costs that must be added to operating budgets. Costs may include all resource categories.
Supportability	Component of the FURPS Model. The level of support required to support a product or service. Generally defined in terms of time, costs and resources.
Sustainment of a Social Venture	How will the Social Venture sustain operations? What is the step-by-step plan to become self-sustaining over time? Consider products and services that can be produced for profit by the individuals benefitting from your Social Venture.
SWOT	Analyze external opportunities and threats based on internal strengths and weaknesses.
Target	A step in the marketing S-T-P process. How will you reach out to the segment you wish to reach? Will you use word of mouth, social media, radio, television, etc.?

Term	Definition
Target Driven	Component of SMARTWAY. Show how the results you deliver will impact the corporation or organization in a timely manner. Responds to the Business Case "When" question.
Teamwork	Positive team building creates an environment of trust and improves performance. Some projects enhance teamwork. Potential benefits area impacting the Balanced Scorecard employee perspective.
Three-Point Estimating	A method of estimating that calculates the best estimate based on pessimistic, most likely, and optimistic estimates. Includes averaging and weighted PERT methods.
Total Cost of Ownership (TCO)	Also referred to as Life Cycle Costing. TCO develops a project costing model that includes support costs for the product or service after the project is complete. The support timeframe is normally designated; i.e. six months.
Total Quality Management	A philosophy that promotes continual process improvement in an effort to improve efficiency and effectiveness, and reduce waste and performance of non-value added activities.
Traceability	All objectives should be linked with corporate or organizational goals and objectives. Traceability shows the linkage.
Training	Training with business value that enhances skills and core competencies critical to organizational success.
Training Costs	Costs required providing key stakeholders with necessary skills to plan, execute, and support a product or service.
Transference (Transfer)	Risk response that transfers accountability and responsibility of a negative risk to a third-party. The third-party actually performs the work or takes accountability. There is normally a cost incurred.
Travel Costs	Costs to pay for project related travel costs. Generally an OPEX expense.

Term	Definition
Trigger	An early warning sign that a risk is about to occur. Initiates a Contingent Response Strategy.
Unique Selling Position (USP)	A quality that places your product, service, or idea above the rest. Something you offer that competitors cannot.
Unknown Risks	Risks you have yet to identify that may impact your Business Case or project.
Usability	Component of the FURPS Model. The ability of a customer to conveniently access the functionality of a product or service.
Variable Costs	Any costs incurred that are production based. For example, if you produce CD's, there is a variable cost for each CD you use. If you produce no CD's, there are no variable costs incurred.
Voice of the Customer (VOC)	The process of reaching out to your customers for feedback. Goal is to understand and satisfy customer needs.
Watch List	Identified risks with a relatively low Risk Score. Generally risks on the "Watch List" are monitored. They are not aggressively managed.
Work Breakdown Structure (WBS)	A WBS defines the activities a project must execute at summary, control account, or work package levels. The WBS also defines the nature of a project as first of its kind or recurring.
Work Life Integration	Some projects enhance overall employee Work Life Integration which leads to increased morale and creativity. Sometimes referred to as "Work Life Balance."

Term	Definition
Worth Implementing	Component of SMARTWAY. Shows how the project you propose in a Business Case will add value. Quantifies the benefits.
Yield Results	Component of SMARTWAY. Set a goal of making reasonable claims that the project you propose can keep. In addition, outline your plan on how you will track and prove that the benefits promised were actually delivered.

Appendix C: Index by Chapter

Topic	Chapter (s)
Adoption	3, 5
AIDA (Awareness, Interest, Desire, Action)	10
Architectural Impact	6
Automation	3
Balanced Scorecard Model	3
Balanced Scorecard: Customer Perspective	3, 5, 6, 10
Balanced Scorecard: Employee or Innovation and Learning Perspective	3, 5, 6, 10
Balanced Scorecard: Financial Perspective	3, 5, 6, 10
Balanced Scorecard: Internal Business or Process Perspective	3, 5, 6, 10
Brainstorming	7
Bookable	3
Business Case Development Flow	1
Business Continuance/Disaster Recovery (BC/DR)	5
Capital Expenses (CAPEX)	4
Cash Flow Diagram	4, 10
Common Business Case Objectives	2
Competitive Advantage	3, 5
Complaints Management	3, 5
Compliance/Legal	3, 5
Connections	10
Contingency Funds	4
Core Competencies	3, 5
Corporate Social Responsibility	10
Cost Avoidance	3, 5
Cost Savings	3, 5
Creativity	3, 5

Topic	Chapter (s)
Critical Success Factor (CSF)	7
Cultural Liaison	10
Customer Satisfaction (CSAT)	3, 5
Customer Partnership Experience (CPE)	3, 5
Define Costs and Benefits	1, 4, 10
Define Objectives	1, 2, 10
Define Risks	1, 5, 10
Define Value Proposition	1, 3, 10
Definitive Statement	9
Delphi Technique	7
Depreciation	4
Develop Executive Summary	1, 8
Devil's Advocate Approach	9
Direct Costs	4, 10
Discount Rate	4
DMAIC	1, 9
Earnings per Share (EPS)	3, 5
Effective Presenting: Attention	9
Effective Presenting: Body	9
Effective Presenting: Conclusion and Next Steps	9
Effective Presenting: Motivation and Overview	9
Effective Presenting: Remotivation	9
Effectiveness	3, 5
Efficiency	3, 5
Emergenetics ®	9
Emergenetics Thinking Attributes: Analytical	9
Emergenetics Thinking Attributes: Conceptual	9
Emergenetics Thinking Attributes: Social	9

Topic	Chapter (s)
Morale and Passion	3, 5
Negative Risks or Threats	5, 10
Net Present Value (NPV)	4
Nominal Group Technique	7
NSAT	3, 5
One-Point Estimating	4
Operational Expenses (OPEX)	4
Pareto Chart	7
Payback	4
Performance Scoring Options	7
Personal Balanced Scorecard Model	11
Personal Balanced Scorecard: Individual Family and Spiritual Perspective	11
Personal Balanced Scorecard: Individual Financial Perspective	11
Personal Balanced Scorecard: Individual Process and Health Perspective	11
Personal Balanced Scorecard: Individual Social Perspective	11
PIE Model (Persuade, Inform, Entertain)	9
Politics	5, 10
Portfolio/Program Support	3, 5
Positive Risks or Opportunities	5, 10
Post Implementation Tracking Plan	6
Potential Cost Categories	4
Presentation Template: 5W+H	8
Presentation Template: OTP	8, 9
Presentation Template: PIP	8, 9
Presentation Template: PNP	8, 9
Presentation Template: PSB	8, 9
Presentation Template: STP	8, 9

Topic	Chapter (s)
Risk Response: Transfer	5
Risk Score	5
Robert S. Kaplan and David P. Norton	3
Rule of 3: Options	6
Run Chart	7
Sample Business Case Format	1
Satisfy Shareholders	3, 5, 10
Scalability	10
Schedule Considerations	5, 6, 10
Secondary Risks	5
Segment-Target-Position	10
Service Level Agreement (SLA)	3
Seth Goldman	10
Sigma	4
SMARTWAY Model	2
SMARTWAY: Assignable	2
SMARTWAY: Attainable	2
SMARTWAY: Measurable	2
SMARTWAY: Relevant	2
SMARTWAY: Specific	2
SMARTWAY: Target Driven	2
SMARTWAY: Worth Implementing	2
SMARTWAY: Yield Results	2
Social Entrepreneurship	10
Soft Benefits	4
Sponsorship	6
Stakeholder Register	6
S-T-P (Segment, Target, Position)	10

CPSIA information can be obtained at www.ICGtesting.com
Printed in the USA
BVOW06s2325301014

372787BV00002BA/24/P